MAKING IDEAS HAPPEN

OVERCOMING THE
OBSTACLES BETWEEN
VISION AND REALITY

SCOTT BELSKY

PORTFOLIO / PENGUIN

PORTFOLIO / PENGUIN

Published by the Penguin Group

Penguin Group (USA) Inc., 375 Hudson Street, New York, New York 10014, U.S.A.
Penguin Group (Canada), 90 Eglinton Avenue East, Suite 700, Toronto, Ontario, Canada M4P 2Y3
(a division of Pearson Penguin Canada Inc.)
Penguin Books Ltd, 80 Strand, London WC2R 0RL, England
Penguin Ireland, 25 St. Stephen's Green, Dublin 2, Ireland (a division of Penguin Books Ltd)
Penguin Books Australia Ltd, 250 Camberwell Road, Camberwell, Victoria 3124, Australia
(a division of Pearson Australia Group Pty Ltd)
Penguin Books India Pvt Ltd, 11 Community Centre, Panchsheel Park, New Delhi - 110 017, India
Penguin Group (NZ), 67 Apollo Drive, Rosedale, Auckland 0632, New Zealand
(a division of Pearson New Zealand Ltd)
Penguin Books (South Africa) (Pty) Ltd, 24 Sturdee Avenue, Rosebank, Johannesburg 2196,
South Africa

Penguin Books Ltd, Registered Offices:
80 Strand, London WC2R ORL, England

First published in the United States of America by Portfolio,
a member of Penguin Group (USA) Inc. 2010
This paperback edition with a new afterword published 2012

5   7   9   10   8   6

Photographs on page 95 used by permission of Colin Williams.

THE LIBRARY OF CONGRESS HAS CATALOGED THE HARDCOVER EDITION AS FOLLOWS:

Belsky, Scott.
    Making ideas happen : overcoming the obstacles between vision and reality / Scott Belsky.
        p.   cm.
    Includes index.
    ISBN 978-1-59184-312-2 (hc.)
    ISBN 978-1-59184-411-2 (pbk.)
    1. Creative ability in business.   2. Success in business.   3. Leadership.   I. Title.
    HD53.B437   2010
    658.4'09—dc22   2009041911

Printed in the United States of America
Set in JansonMT
Designed by Neuwirth & Associates, Inc.

To Nancy and Mark,
with gratitude for the
precious opportunity
of endless possibility

Contents

MAKING
IDEAS
HAPPEN

INTRODUCTION:
Making Ideas Happen

IDEAS DON'T HAPPEN because they are great—or by accident. The misconception that great ideas inevitably lead to success has prevailed for too long. Whether you have the perfect solution for an everyday problem or a bold new concept for a creative masterpiece, you must transform vision into reality. Far from being some stroke of creative genius, this capacity to make ideas happen can be developed by anyone. You just need to modify your organizational habits, engage a broader community, and develop your leadership capability.

This book aims to take pie-in-the-sky notions of how the creative process unfolds and bring them down to earth. Creative people are known for winging it: improvising and acting on intuition is, in some way, the haloed essence of what we do and who we are. However, when we closely analyze how the most successful and productive creatives, entrepreneurs, and businesspeople truly make ideas happen, it turns out that "having the idea" is just a small part of the process, perhaps only 1 percent of the journey.

Thomas Edison once famously quipped, "Genius is 1 percent inspiration and 99 percent perspiration." For the creative mind, inspiration comes easily. But what makes up the other 99 percent of making ideas happen? Read on for a surprisingly pragmatic set of insights and tips that have emerged from over six years spent studying the behaviors and skill sets of those who make their ideas happen again and again.

A QUICK PRIMER:
Making Your Ideas Happen

In the sections ahead, we will discuss the methods behind spectacular achievements—ideas that have overcome the odds and become realities. But before we do, here's a primer on a few terms I use throughout the book and some assumptions I make about you (and your ideas)!

You have ideas that you want to make happen. Whatever your business or industry, success is dependent on developing and executing new ideas. We're not just talking about new products, new business ideas, or your vision for the next great American novel. You likely come up with creative solutions to problems every day. Unfortunately, regardless of how great your ideas may be, most of them will never happen. Most ideas get lost in what I call the "project plateau," a period of intense execution where your natural creative tendencies turn against you. As a leader in your industry (and the leader of your life), you must learn to defy these tendencies.

You can develop the capacity to make ideas happen. From years of researching creative individuals and teams, I will share the practices used to make ideas happen, time and time again.

(continued)

Making ideas happen = Ideas + Organization + Communal forces + Leadership capability. There is a framework for all of the insights and methods we will discuss. Aside from generating ideas (which we will not discuss), the capacity to make ideas happen is a combination of the forces of organization, community, and leadership. We will dive into each of these forces and discuss how you should use them in your own creative pursuits.

Organization enables you to manage and ultimately execute your ideas. In the modern world of information overload and constant connectivity, you must manage your energy wisely. Otherwise, you will fall into a state of "reactionary work flow," where you act impulsively (rather than proactively) and simply try to stay afloat. Everything in life should be approached as a project. Every project can be broken down into just three things: Action Steps, Backburner Items, and References. The "Action Method," which we will discuss in the first section of the book, is a composite of the best practices for productivity shared by creative leaders. The Action Method helps those of us with creative tendencies live and work with a bias toward action. With an understanding of this methodology, we will delve deeply into prioritization, managing your energy and attention, and fully executing your ideas.

The forces of community are invaluable and readily available. Ideas don't happen in isolation. You must embrace opportunities to broadcast and then refine your ideas through the energy of those around you. In the second section of this book, we will break down the communal forces that cause ideas to gain traction.

Fruitful innovation requires a unique capacity to lead. Leading any sort of creative pursuit requires an overhaul of how we motivate others and ourselves. The most admired leaders are able to build

(continued)

and manage teams that can overcome the obstacles faced in creative projects. There is also a mind-set we must achieve to withstand (and capitalize on) the doubts and pressures we face along the way.

While the tendency to generate ideas is rather natural, the path to making them happen is tumultuous. This book is intended to outfit you with the methods and insights that build your capacity to defy the odds and make your ideas happen.

Making This Book Happen

I have always been a bit frustrated with creativity. I would get impatient watching colleagues and friends come up with great ideas, only to become distracted by other ideas and the general demands of life. I found the poor odds that anyone would actually follow through with an idea very upsetting. After a series of jobs and a graduate degree, my frustration turned into fascination and subsequently a career aspiration.

Believe it or not, it all started at Goldman Sachs, the investment bank. After an exceedingly dry finance job working with European equities, I was invited to join a group in the firm's executive office known as Pine Street—a small team of professionals dedicated to leadership development and organizational improvement. My focus was on developing the potential of innovative leaders both within the firm and at large clients, including hedge funds and other high-growth companies. This position provided me with a precious opportunity to study (and spread) the best practices of those leaders who were the most effective at executing their ideas.

While identifying and spreading these best practices, I spent a lot of time observing business leaders dealing with the daily struggles of managing people amidst rapid changes in their businesses. At the same time, outside Goldman Sachs, I began to work informally with a variety of creative people in New York City—photographers, entrepreneurs, designers, and so on—to help them master the challenge of following through on their ideas. Their needs, it seemed, were endless.

During my years in Pine Street, I realized that the creative world desperately needed cutting-edge information on productivity and leadership development. Creative professionals—defined as those who generate (and sometimes execute) ideas for a living—constitute what is likely the most disorganized community on the planet. But these same individuals are ultimately responsible for the design, entertainment, literature, and new businesses that bring meaning to our lives. I saw not only an opportunity but also a responsibility to help those with ideas overcome the obstacles to make them happen. As such, I committed my professional life to organizing the creative world.

My experiences inside and outside Goldman Sachs led me to pursue my MBA at Harvard and to simultaneously found Behance, a company dedicated to organizing and empowering the creative world. While at Harvard I was able to explore productivity in the creative industries, particularly during an independent research project with Teresa Amabile, the famed expert on creativity in business and a professor at Harvard Business School. Meanwhile, I assembled a small team of like-minded thinkers in New York City who shared my enthusiasm, curiosity, and desire to organize the creative world.

Launched in 2007, the Behance Network is an online collective of millions of leading creative professionals from around the world. At all hours of the day and night, network members post their latest projects—ranging from designs for major brands, to architectural plans for buildings, to new fashion lines and photographic series—for their peers to review and for potential clients to consider. Millions of visitors explore these projects every month. Each project is a testament to an idea that has been pushed forward.

Behance provides organization, feedback exchange, efficient communication, and promotion to support the careers of creative professionals and boost efficiency in the talent recruitment process. As we tweak the various components of Behance, our guiding mission is to help creative people and teams organize their work, collaborate, and lead others. From the Network's data—and many focus groups—we have gathered insights into how people with ideas gain traction and stay accountable.

Over the years, our team at Behance has continued to research and develop methods and tools for creative leaders. We transformed the tips and insights of the Action Method into a suite of paper products. In 2009, we launched The 99U Conference and online "university" as an exchange for tips and insights about the execution of ideas and leading productive creative careers.

My team's passionate pursuit is to understand why and how some people and organizations are consistently able to push ideas to fruition, while most others do so haphazardly or not at all. We have interviewed hundreds of the individuals and teams that make life interesting—leading designers, emerging technology teams, media executives, writers, serial entrepreneurs, filmmakers, and everything in between. We never ask typical questions such as "What inspires you?" or "Where do your ideas come from?" On the contrary, we focus less on the creativity and more on how these people stay productive and consistently execute their ideas.

Along the way we have met with teams at revered companies across industries, including Apple, IDEO, Disney, Google, Zappos, and Facebook, as well as with brilliant individuals such as Stefan Sagmeister, Seth Godin, and Chris Anderson, who have, through their consistent execution of ideas, become admired thought leaders in the creative world. We learned that these teams and individuals did not arrive at success through a mysterious spark of creative genius. Rather, the people who consistently make ideas happen utilize many of the same best practices.

Specifically, we discovered that the most productive creative individuals and teams have a lot in common when it comes to (1) organization and relentless execution, (2) engaging peers and leveraging communal forces, and (3) strategies for leading creative pursuits. While many of us spend too much energy searching for the next great idea, my research shows that we would be better served by developing the capacity to make ideas happen—a capacity that endures over time.

My hope is that the insights in this book will provide you with a road map for building that capacity—and ultimately help more great ideas gain traction. The era upon us is filled with problems and opportunities that require fresh innovation like never before. Being more efficient or cheaper is no longer enough to be competitive in a global marketplace. We need to conceive new ideas to address the problems and opportunities that surround us—and we need to defy the odds and make these ideas actually happen.

This book was written with the creative person or team in mind—people driven by deep interests and gifted with multiple ideas on how to pursue them. But this book was not written merely for the stereotypical "artist." John Maeda, president of the Rhode Island School of Design, put it best: "I'm not for the notion of 'artistic' or 'creative' meaning making a pretty picture. Every entrepreneur I have ever met is an artist. They are all forced to become comfortable with failure. And for entrepreneurs, their canvas is their company."

Why Most Ideas Never Happen

It is a shame that countless ideas with the potential to transform our lives—concepts for new drug discoveries, models for new businesses, inklings for musical masterpieces, sketches for iconic pieces of art—are conceived and squandered in the hands of creative geniuses every day. The ideas that move industries forward are not the result of tremendous creative insight but rather of masterful stewardship. Yes, there is a method to the madness of turning an idea into a reality—it's just not as romantic as you thought.

The Life and Death of Ideas

Creativity is the catalyst for brilliant accomplishments, but it is also the greatest obstacle. If you examine the natural course of a new idea—from conception to execution—you'll see that nearly all new ideas die a premature death. If that seems far-fetched, just consider the ideas that you have conceived on your own but never implemented: a novel you wanted to write, a business project you wanted to launch, a restaurant you wanted to open. For most of us the list goes on and on. New ideas face an uphill battle from the moment they are conceived.

The cynics might suggest that the death of most ideas is actually a good thing. After all, from a day-to-day perspective, society appears to thrive on conformity. The status quo is the oil in the gears of society; it keeps us all happy and healthy. Even the companies that preach innovation still need to satisfy existing customers, meet their earnings targets, and keep the lights on. To a degree, the natural immune system that extinguishes new ideas in big companies is essential. After all, fresh ideas have the potential to take us off course; they are seldom economical (at first) and introduce tremendous risk to a finely tuned system. So it is with good reason that every new idea faces a battery of external obstacles before it even has a chance of materializing. Sadly, these obstacles don't discriminate between good and bad ideas.

Even more powerful than the obstacles around us, however, are the obstacles within us. The most potent forces that kill off new ideas are our own limitations. Time is very limited, and with the demands of family, friends, work, and sleep, most ideas lose traction immediately. If your idea survives the honeymoon period of excitement, it may still be forgotten because you are probably the only one who knows about it. Most ideas are born and lost in isolation.

Even if you do possess the single-minded focus necessary to pursue a particular idea, your journey forward will be full of battles. Whether you work alone or with a team, you will become mired in the challenge of staying productive, accountable, and in control. These journeys are physically and psychologically exhausting, and the road is littered with the carcasses of half-baked ideas that were abandoned or surrendered along the way. It is a tragic truth that most new ideas, despite their quality and importance, will never see the light of day.

Fortunately, there's another side to this story. Across every industry and in every creative pursuit, there are some people who are consistently good at both generating and executing their ideas. This book captures how they do it.

The Creative's Conundrum: At Odds with Our Very Essence

The prospect of making ideas happen carries with it a special conundrum. The forces that help us be productive and execute our ideas are often at odds with the very source of our ideas: our creativity.

To get a sense of what it's like to live governed by our creative side, look no further than Chad and Risa—two people I met early on who suffered from many of the common ailments that plague creative people.

A well-known production head at a top film studio was in despair as he told me about Chad, one of the most gifted screenwriters he had ever met. Chad spent his days and nights writing. He'd had a few decent films, but he had written many more misses than hits and cycled through more than a few agents. Chad checked his e-mail "every week or so." Production executives and Chad's close friends said the same thing: Chad is tough to get in touch with and is extremely disorganized. He is unable to stay on top of his ideas, some of which have the potential to fit into various projects.

"Plot twists come and leave my mind every day," Chad lamented to me.

As I talked to him about his struggle to stay organized, Chad grew defensive. He reminded me that he was a writer, he loved his job, and that writing was what he does best.

"Writing is chaos, and writing is my essence," Chad proclaimed.

But then Chad admitted wondering what benefits he might realize if he got his "stuff in order."

A new approach to organization made all the difference. Chad needed a system that would capture all of his fledgling ideas but also channel his energy toward the projects that required action. A self-proclaimed "technophobe," Chad created a paper-based system that displayed the Action Steps for his most important projects in plain sight. He stopped living his life at the mercy of Post-it notes and trying to keep up with e-mail. Instead, he adopted a set of principles and even a few rituals that made him focus on the actionable aspects of his most important projects without abandoning his creative process. After a full introduction to the Action Method, you too will start to reconsider your own approach to organization in personal and professional projects.

And now, a quick glimpse into Risa's life. As a student of human behavior, philosophy enthusiast, and relentless thinker, Risa spent years working on a new theory about the social development of parentless children. While her ideas filled hundreds of pages of notes, she had yet to pull the project together when I first met her. She would only share her ideas with a few people and seldom review her own writing, always preferring to tackle something new. She didn't care much for feedback, but she would talk for hours about the need for her work and the broad applicability of her findings. Without a doubt, Risa was an extremely passionate and talented woman.

Along the way, Risa had hopped from job to job. Her voice was reduced to shaky disappointment as she tried to make sense of the half-baked projects that had accumulated over the years. "Nothing has happened yet for me," she admitted. Amidst a surplus of possible excuses, Risa was unable to explain exactly what was stalling her progress. She was failing to make any of her ideas happen.

Risa was a brilliant mind left to her own devices. Without others to challenge her ideas and hold her accountable, she was struggling. The turning point for Risa involved setting up a blog, engaging a dear friend who became a mentor, and joining a local philosophy forum where she could exchange her ideas with others on a weekly basis. Her scattered ideas became a more focused set of projects. Eventually, Risa's years of research resulted in a published book that received much fanfare. For Risa, the forces of community made all the difference.

Chad's and Risa's stories showcase some of the common struggles of the creative mind. Making ideas happen often comes down to a battle against our own essence. Having a brilliant creative mind won't cut it.

In this book, I will focus on creative leaders and teams across industries that, time and time again, make their ideas happen. One such leader is Jonathan Harris. A unique hybrid of artist, intellectual, and technologist, Harris is best described as a storyteller and Internet anthropologist. He may have graduated from Princeton, but there is nothing traditional about his career. Jonathan's passion, as he describes it, is to pursue ideas that "begin with really basic questions about the world" and explore "the role of stories as time capsules."

Such a broad passion might be dismissed as typical go-nowhere creative ambition. But Jonathan has been exceptionally productive in his creative endeavors. Before the age of twenty-eight, he launched multiple award-winning Web productions that pushed the envelope of human interaction with technology. His projects—"We Feel Fine," a global online experiment in human emotion that allows you to observe thousands of people expressing a common feeling at once; "Phylotaxis," an exploration of the intersection of science and culture; and the critically acclaimed "Whale Hunt," a photo documentary that employed a head-mounted camera that automatically captured photographs every few minutes during an Alaska whale-hunting trip—were all ideas that actually happened.

Jonathan's work has been featured on CNN and the BBC, and in *Wired*, and exhibited at Le Centre Pompidou in Paris and the Museum of Modern Art in New York. In short, Jonathan is not hampered by his ceaseless flow of ideas. At a glance, his ideas might seem too lofty or avant-garde to gain traction. But they consistently defy the odds. Jonathan gives his ideas every chance to succeed by pushing them to fruition.

"I think there are two phases," Jonathan explained to me, "the first being the one where you are just picking up signals from the ether. [Ideas] aggregate over time and then pop out one day when you are in the shower. I think the second phase is deciding 'Okay, I'm going to actually pursue this given thing.' And then once you've decided, it's a different mind-set from that point forward. At least with that particular idea, because you have to become more rational and more logical, more disciplined. It's less about receiving and it's more about synthesizing and distilling and then ultimately producing. And I think it's something that a lot of creative people struggle with because maybe the former is a more pleasing way to live your life, but the latter is the only way that you actually get anything done."

Jonathan believes that any successful creative entity must be comfortable alternating between these two creative phases: ideation and execution. When Jonathan starts talking about his approach to projects and work flow, you immediately sense the value he places on self-discipline and simplicity. You also realize that Jonathan begins a project with serious expectations for its viability with an audience. While his work is personally fulfilling, its true purpose is to reach other people.

Many claim they create solely for themselves; they argue that the conception and actualization of an idea is simply a means for self-fulfillment and nothing more. But this argument is selfish: an idea executed for an audience of one is an awful waste of potential inspiration and value for the greater good.

"I think that if you want to treat your work like a virus that will reach a lot of people," Jonathan explained, "it's good to package it in a way that can optimize the number of people it can reach, and that can mean different things. You can make something really, really palatable and turn it into an HBO miniseries or you can make something moderately palatable and turn it into something that goes into an art museum or you can make something not at all palatable and turn it into something you do in your basement."

Jonathan is just another member of the powerful cadre of creative professionals who have been able to overcome the challenges posed by the creative psyche. The attributes that Jonathan embodies are common among people who routinely push ideas to fruition.

The most exceptional creative leaders and teams who I have met are able to generate a surplus of ideas with discipline and poise. They ground their creative energy with a supreme sense of organization.

As professionals, they have overcome the stigma of self-marketing and use their respective communities to stay accountable. And as leaders, they are able to build and lead teams that thrive over time.

The quality of ideas themselves is less important than the platform upon which they materialize. Realize that you control the platform for your ideas.

The Forces That Make Ideas Happen

This book is divided into three sections, each presenting a critical set of tools for making ideas happen: Organization and Execution, the Forces of Community, and Leadership Capability. Of course, there is also the idea itself—the catalyst. But, for the purposes of this book, I will leave the creative inspiration and ideas up to you.

> **MAKING IDEAS HAPPEN = *(THE IDEA)* + ORGANIZATION AND EXECUTION + FORCES OF COMMUNITY + LEADERSHIP CAPABILITY**

The capacity to make ideas happen is defined by the confluence of the three core components outlined in the equation shown here. Reaching your greatest potential requires mastering the intricate balance of all three forces at play—whether you are executing an idea on your own or working with a team.

Let's quickly discuss the relevance of the three components:

Organization and execution. It is undeniable that your approach to productivity largely determines your creative output. The way you organize projects, prioritize, and manage your energy is arguably more important than the quality of the ideas you wish to pursue. There is nothing new in this assertion. The necessity of staying organized has been well-documented in innumerable books. Our thirst for a simple solution is evident in the huge success of methodology-oriented books and productivity blogs.

Few, however, have explored organization and execution within the context of the creative mind, or within the context of our rapidly changing work environment. Creatives have always represented one of the most mobile groups in the workforce, and this trend of mobility is now extending to the business world at large.

The ranks of freelance, contract, and part-time workers as well as small-business owners are increasing daily. Many businesses are hiring people for rotational programs that last only two years. Practices such as "daylighting"—in which an employee works on a creative, personal project for 10–20 percent of their at-work time—are increasing in popularity as companies like Google tout their effectiveness. Even the more traditional "lifer" companies, such as General Electric and IBM, are acknowledging the value of a shorter experiential education over a lifelong career opportunity.

What this means is that, regardless of your industry, your professional life is becoming more nomadic, digital, and flexible. But as a wise sage once said—and what every small-business owner knows all too well—"total freedom means total responsibility." As where and how you work become more flexible, the onus of organization shifts increasingly onto the individual. As such, productivity is not about how efficient you are at work. Instead, your productivity is really about how well you are able to make an impact in what matters most to you.

You might wonder, "How can I stay organized amidst the everyday chaos of accomplishing tasks, managing projects, and staying mentally clear enough to still be creative?" There are surprisingly practical methods and tricks that can, collectively, become your controls for making ideas happen. As we discuss examples and common themes of the especially productive, you will come to see that it is at the intersection of creative energy and organizational prowess where great ideas become actions and ultimately revolutionary achievements.

Leveraging communal forces. I have found that, across the board, extremely productive and accomplished people and teams capitalize on the power of community to push their ideas forward. The utilization of communal forces yields invaluable feedback and idea refinement, builds and nourishes beneficial relationships, and establishes a connective tissue that provides resources, support, and inspiration.

As psychologist Keith Sawyer, a protégé of Mihaly Csikszentmihalyi (author of the renowned creativity book *Flow: The Psychology of Optimal Experience*), writes in his 2007 book *Group Genius*, "All great inventions emerge from a long sequence of small sparks; the first idea often isn't all that good, but thanks to collaboration it later sparks another idea, or it's reinterpreted in an unexpected way. Collaboration brings small sparks together to generate breakthrough innovation."

Even if the notion of the lone creative genius existed in the past (and Sawyer would argue that it did not), there can be no doubt that it's wildly outdated in the twenty-first century. The hyperconnectivity made possible by the Internet has acted as a massive accelerator for the "small sparks" that fuel the refinement of ideas. Nearly every individual or company I've spoken with has harnessed the power of the Web to achieve many of the goals we'll discuss in this section: gathering feedback, honing ideas, increasing transparency, and sharing and promoting completed work.

We'll look at, among other examples, how Zappos CEO Tony Hsieh uses Twitter to increase transparency and find inspiration, how best-selling author and *Wired* editor in chief Chris Anderson uses a community of engaged readers to refine his groundbreaking theorems, and how marketing strategist Noah Brier gathers feedback to improve his Web experiments.

Of course, the Internet is just one means of accessing and building your community. The concepts and insights that I'll be discussing are not tied to any single medium—and they can be applied in a number of ways depending on your personality and what works best for you.

But whatever your disposition, I cannot stress enough the importance of tapping into the communal forces around you: community opens the door to new approaches for old challenges and spurs a more informed and powerful creative instinct. Accountability, one of the most crucial benefits of engaging with your community, is what binds you to the relentless pursuit of your ideas. As you become accountable to others, your creative impulses become tangible projects. Your ideas grow roots. Community strengthens both your creative energy and your commitment to channel it.

Leadership in creative pursuits. History is made by passionate, creative people and organizations with the rare ability to lead others— and themselves. Leadership capability is what makes the pursuit of an idea sustainable, scalable, and ultimately successful. Unfortunately, there is a huge void of leadership capability in the creative world, as evidenced by the high attrition and frequent management debacles across the creative industries. When employees quit a creative team, it is most often a result of an interpersonal conflict or not feeling engaged by the subject matter; it is rarely about money.* To grow and sustain creative pursuits, you must be able to keep others engaged with your ideas.

Leadership capability relates both to your leadership of others as well as to your ability to lead yourself. Perhaps some of the greatest hurdles in implementing ideas are personal deficiencies—common

---

* Anecdotally, I have spoken with multiple human resources professionals within creative agencies who report that the most common reasons for quitting, as stated in exit interviews, are related to management or morale issues rather than more competitive salaries.

psychological barriers that creative minds often face when executing ideas. Very few of the famously prolific and productive creative people we discuss in this book are "naturals." While the ideas might flow generously, the methods behind the capacity to make ideas happen are often counterintuitive. In some ways, the self-discipline and restraints necessary to execute an idea can feel like a tremendous compromise of your very essence as a creative person.

I have come to call this notion the "creative's compromise" because you must be prepared to adopt new restraints and best practices that—at first—feel uncomfortable. You will never need to compromise your morals or artistic integrity, but you will need to exert control over your destructive tendencies. Perhaps you have the tendency to jump from idea to idea to idea without ever following through on any particular one. Or maybe you have the tendency to incubate ideas privately. You might be avoiding feedback for fear of criticism, and when you do receive it, you may subconsciously find ways to discount it. Everyone with the gift of creativity has a series of tendencies that can become obstacles. The journey to a more productive life as a creative leader starts with a candid self-assessment of who you are, your tendencies, and the greatest barriers before you.

You need to think differently about how you manage your ideas, your community of collaborators, and yourself. As we discuss leadership in the context of creative pursuits, we will reconsider the rewards systems that govern our own actions and discuss how to manage the delicate chemistry of a creative team.

A Final Note As We Begin

Of course, even if you were to adopt all of the best practices in this book, making ideas happen will never be easy. Across the hundreds of interviews conducted during the research for this book, no individual or team I met was without frustration. Anything new inherently works against the grain. And working against the grain is uncomfortable. The aspiration you should have is to improve your approach. And the responsibility you should feel is to give your ideas a chance.

This book is highly practical, filled with methods that have worked for others. Every tip and insight is kept short and actionable, so you can put this book to use right away and return to it as a resource when you face different challenges throughout your career. You will find some sections more mechanical than others. Keep in mind that execution isn't pretty. However, your effort to develop the capacity to make ideas happen is a worthy investment. The best practices presented here are yours to digest, scrutinize, and modify as you see fit. My hope is that you take away a few crucial realizations that make all the difference.

The conversation also continues online, where a network of thousands of creative people and teams, like you, are eager to push their ideas forward. As our research evolves online at our think tank (the99percent.com) and at the Behance Network (behance.net), I hope you'll both learn from the material and become a contributor.

Let's get started!

1 ORGANIZATION AND EXECUTION

My freedom thus consists in my moving about within the narrow frame that I have assigned to myself for each one of my undertakings. I shall go even further: my freedom will be so much the greater and more meaningful the more narrowly I limit my field of action and the more I surround myself with obstacles. Whatever diminishes constraint diminishes strength. The more constraints one imposes, the more one frees oneself of the claims that shackle the spirit.

—Igor Stravinsky, *Poetics of Music in the Form of Six Lessons*

IN A WORLD obsessed with innovation, it is easy to fall in love with ideas. The creativity quotient is the darling of the adventurous mind. For some of us, creativity is intoxicating. Our society has gone so far as to divide its members into two camps, the "left-brain people" and the "right-brain people," under a radical (and arguably false) assumption that both parts of the brain cannot coexist effectively— that brilliant creative people are inherently unable to act as organizers and leaders. But they can. And when creative and organizational tendencies are able to coexist, society is pushed forward as remarkable ideas are actualized. The real problem is less about how society views creative people and more about how creative people view themselves.

In 2007, Behance conducted a poll of over a thousand self-described "creative professionals," asking them how organized they considered themselves to be. Only 7 percent of those who responded claimed to feel "very organized." Double that number (14 percent) claimed to work in a state of "utter chaos," and the largest group attested to "more mess than order" (48 percent). Upon further follow-up, I also observed that, far from being a point of concern, the disarray experienced by many of these professionals was regarded as a badge of honor!

The reality is that creative environments—and the creative psyche itself—are not conducive to organization. We become intolerant of procedures, restrictions, and process. Nevertheless, organization is the guiding force of productivity: if you want to make an idea happen, you need to have a process for doing so.

Part of the creative mind's rebellion is understandable, because there is no one best process for developing ideas and then making them happen. *Process* in general has a bad reputation; anyone who has worked in a corporate bureaucracy knows why. When a process is imposed on you externally, it can weigh you down and diminish your energy. Process is a deeply personal matter of taste and habit, especially for creative people. Your process works best for you when it is customized to your own personal preferences.

Rather than ask you to emulate a static process that works for others, I will instead present you with a set of core elements to strengthen your existing process. Admired creative leaders share a common approach to organization and managing projects. In this section of the book, you will hear from some especially productive creative leaders and firms—people like prolific author Seth Godin and legendary designer and college president John Maeda. We will also discuss some of the lesser-known—but extremely powerful—practices used at companies famous for innovation, such as IDEO, Walker Digital, and Disney.

THE COMPETITIVE ADVANTAGE OF ORGANIZATION

ORGANIZATION IS ALL about applying order to the many elements of a creative project. There are concepts you hope to retain, resources you want to utilize, and then the components of the project itself—stuff that needs to get done and other stuff that needs to be referred back to. There are also external elements like deadlines, budgets, clients, and other constraints. All of these elements combine (or collide) as you seek to create, develop, and execute ideas.

These elements exist in any creative project, but we don't always acknowledge them. Often we try to work around them (or ignore them). Of course, doing so decreases the odds that our ideas will ever happen.

The most important, and most often neglected, organizational element is structure. We tend to shun structure as a way of protecting the free-flowing nature of ideas. But without structure, our ideas fail to build upon one another. Structure enables us to capture our ideas and arrange them in a way that helps us (and others) relate to them.

Without structure, we can't focus long enough on any particular idea to find its weaknesses. Ideas that should be killed will linger, and others that require development may be forgotten. Structure helps us achieve a tangible outcome from our ideas.

Structure and organization are worthy of serious discussion because they provide a competitive advantage. Only through organization can we seize the benefits from bursts of creativity. If you develop the capacity to organize yourself and those around you, you can beat the odds.

Your Approach to Organization and the Destiny of Your Ideas

Supply chain management is a heavily logistical aspect of business that seldom attracts much fanfare. Companies like Wal-Mart and Toyota are legendary for how well they distribute and manage inventory. There is no debate that the mechanics of a company—especially its supply chain management practices—help determine the costs, quality, and availability of the product. There are consulting firms and executive-level positions within companies dedicated entirely to managing the supply chain—the embodiment of organization within a company. At the same time, many of us don't really associate such tasks with creativity and ideas.

Since 2004, AMR Research, a leading authority on supply chain research that serves numerous Fortune 500 companies, has published an annual list of the twenty-five companies with the best supply chain management. You might be surprised to learn that Apple debuted on the list at No. 2 in 2007, and overtook companies such as Anheuser-Busch, Wal-Mart, Procter & Gamble, and Toyota to take the No. 1 slot in 2008.

Why would Apple, a company known for new ideas and its ability to "think different," also be one of the most organized companies on the planet? The answer is that—like it or not—organization is a major force for making ideas happen.

Organization is just as important as ideas when it comes to making an impact. Consider the following equation:

CREATIVITY X ORGANIZATION = IMPACT

If the impact of our ideas is, in fact, largely determined by our ability to stay organized, then we would observe that those with tons of creativity but little to no organization yield, on average, nothing. Let's imagine a wildly creative but totally disorganized thinker; the equation would be:

100 X 0 = 0

Does this bring someone to mind? Someone who has loads of ideas but is so disorganized that no one particular idea is ever fully realized? You could argue that someone with half the creativity and just a little more organizational ability would make a great deal more impact:

50 X 2 = 100

The equation helps us understand why some "less-creative" artists might produce more work than their talented and inventive peers. A shocking and perhaps unfortunate realization emerges: someone with average creativity but stellar organizational skills will make a greater impact than the disorganized creative geniuses among us. I'll ask you to reserve artistic judgment while we consider a few examples.

If you have ever passed through a resort town in America (and, increasingly, abroad), you may have come across a storefront gallery for Thomas Kinkade, "Painter of Light." Similarly, if you are an avid reader, air traveler, or subscriber to fiction book clubs, you have likely come across one of the many novels by James Patterson. Both Kinkade and Patterson are examples of creatives who have generated impressively large bodies of work. It is known that both Kinkade and Patterson employ many people to assist in the production and distribution of their work. In this regard, they are leaders of large enterprises. However, while Kinkade and Patterson have large fan bases, they are also consistently maligned by critics in their industries for being particularly unimaginative and productive to a fault.

Patterson holds the *New York Times* Best Sellers record with thirty-nine best-selling titles. His Web site notes that in 2007, one out of every fifteen hardcover novels sold was a Patterson book. The author has sold over 150 million copies of his books worldwide. His abundant outreach campaigns include marketing programs such as the "James Patterson PageTurner Awards," and many of his dozens of published books have been optioned for television series and movies. Not surprisingly, he has started his own firm, James Patterson Entertainment, and is known to work on more than five novels at once.

In the industry newsletter *Publishers Lunch*, it was noted that if Patterson were treated as his own publishing house, "he'd be tied for fourth for most #1 bestsellers in 2006—ahead of HarperCollins, a major publisher." It is no surprise that critics have likened Patterson's creative process to a factory. Patrick Anderson, a well-known critic for the *Washington Post*, described Patterson in one review as "the absolute pits, the lowest common denominator of cynical, skuzzy, assembly-line writing." Other critics have lambasted the similarity of the plots of his novels.

As for Patterson's take on his success, he attributes it to a "golden gut—an ability to sense what's going to appeal to a lot of people." Patterson's stunning productivity may stem from his previous life. Before authoring his first novel, Patterson was the CEO of J. Walter Thompson, one of the world's top ad agencies. Climbing the ladder to CEO, he developed the strengths as a leader and organizer that have distinguished his performance as a writer. Regardless of what the critics say, Patterson makes ideas happen at an almost alarming rate. And despite what you may think of his ideas, he is undeniably prolific and consistent. In our Creativity × Organization equation, he is either a 50×100 or a 100×100, and his impact is nothing short of remarkable.

Thomas Kinkade is similarly prolific. The sheer number of paintings coming out of Kinkade's studio is bewildering. In Kinkade's case, some may argue that many of his pieces look the same or are reused for different purposes. Kinkade's work is described in one book, *The Rebel Sell*, as "so awful it must be seen to be believed." There are even comedy Web sites that parody the work for being cliché and mass produced. One might argue that Kinkade's work is short on fresh ideas, but it is produced, marketed, and distributed efficiently and successfully.

In our Creativity × Organization = Impact equation, both Patterson and Kinkade are exceptionally high on the organization side and have made an incredible impact in their respective industries as a result. From this you can see that the "organization" side of the equation deserves as much focus as the "creativity" side. Why? Because ultimately you want to make an impact with your ideas.

Apple, Kinkade, and Patterson are just a few examples of the power of the organization part of the equation. Amidst the joy of generating ideas, it is worth taking the time to develop your ability to organize them—and the resources required to stay organized.

The notion of spending energy moving stuff around rather than creating new stuff is understandably unappealing to the creative mind. Rather than forcing something that is not natural, we must understand the value of organization and develop creative approaches to it.

THE ACTION METHOD:
Work and Life with a Bias Toward Action

WHEN BRAINSTORMING, WE generate ideas to solve problems—or conceive of something entirely new. Once an idea is posed, it is played with and expanded upon without limits. Each question and extrapolation gives rise to alternative and tangential ideas. An intoxicating creative exchange commences that often leads to unexpected places.

But the harsh reality is that brainstorming sessions often yield disappointing results. Ideas with great potential fade from the participants' minds with each additional idea thrown into the mix. Strong possibilities are trumped by alternative—not necessarily better—possibilities. Ultimately, we surrender to the clock, our takeaway being either the last idea mentioned or the consensus idea—a watered-down version of an early idea that kept coming up again and again. We go back to our desks with a mishmash of notes and sketches, often with no sense of who should do what, what happens when, and what else needs to be researched or discussed before action can be taken.

A surplus of ideas is as dangerous as a drought. The tendency to jump from idea to idea to idea spreads your energy horizontally rather than vertically. As a result, you'll struggle to make progress. In a no-holds-barred session of blue-sky brainstorming, rampant idea exchange is exhilarating. But without some structure, you can become an addict of the brain-spinning indulgence of idea generation.

Recognizing the tendency to bask in idea generation is the first step toward managing your energy to ensure a tangible outcome. While you may enjoy generating brilliant ideas and imagining new possibilities, you must approach every occasion of creativity with a dose of skepticism and a bias toward action. Brainstorming should start with a question and the goal of capturing something specific, relevant, and actionable. You should depart such sessions with more conviction than when you started.

Randall Stutman, an executive coach for some of the most senior leaders in corporate America, often says that the greatest leaders are "optimistic about the future, but pessimistic about tasks." In the creative world, leaders should be excited about the potential of new ideas, but they should also be deeply concerned with how to manage their ideas as projects.

Ultimately, every idea is associated with a project. Whether personal (a birthday party you are planning) or professional (a new product launch), every project revolves around ideas that you want to push into action.

Brace yourself; we're about to get our hands dirty. The term "project management" makes most creative people cringe. Elaborate Gantt charts and byzantine procedures plague bureaucracies large and small. Depending on your approach and your mind-set, the experience of organizing and managing a project can be miserable or deeply satisfying. Nevertheless, ideas are made to happen only as the result of a well-managed work flow. So, bear with me as I make the case for how you should manage your many projects.

My team and I have observed how hundreds of individuals and teams manage projects. Over the years, we have aggregated the best practices and developed a method for creative project management that works across the spectrum—from the smallest personal task to massive corporate endeavors involving hundreds of participants and dozens of milestones. The "Action Method" can be grasped and adopted by even the most wayward creative minds.

Reconsider How You Manage Projects

The Action Method causes us to question many of the traditional practices of project management. Handling a project as some big and dense objective laid out by the higher-ups and distributed to the masses is no longer ideal. In the pursuit of making ideas happen, the traditional emphasis on planning and constant top-down communication is bulky and counterproductive.

We have found that even within large bureaucratic companies with elaborate, formal project management systems, the most productive people run their own parallel processes to accomplish projects more flexibly. These homegrown systems share a common set of principles:

A relentless bias toward action pushes ideas forward. Most ideas come and go while the matter of follow-up is left to chance. Next steps are often lost amidst a mishmash of notes and sketches, and typical creative tools like plain blank notebooks only contribute to the problem. For each idea, you must capture and highlight your "Action Steps."

Stuff that is actionable must be made personal. Putting one person in charge of managing next steps tends to not work. Making one person responsible for taking the notes and then sending them around to team members makes project responsibilities vague and impersonal. Each person needs to "own" their Action Steps. When tasks are written in your own handwriting, in your own idiom, they remain familiar and are more likely to be executed.

Taking and organizing extensive notes aren't worth the effort. We have found that notes are seldom used and can actually get in the way of capturing and following up on Action Steps. The process of excessive note taking actually interferes with the bias toward action that is necessary for a productive creative environment. If you simply capture and then tend to the actions required for a project, you are already way ahead of the game.

Use design-centric systems to stay organized. The color, texture, size, and style of the materials used to capture Action Steps are important. People who have successfully developed personal systems for productivity over the years claim that their designs make their Action Steps more appealing (and thus more likely to be taken).

Organize in the context of projects, not location. These days, your work doesn't necessarily always happen at the office. Productivity is not about managing a single in-box or keeping different lists of what should be done "at work" or "at home." Rather than using a location-centric approach to work flow and scheduling, we have found that a project-centric approach to productivity is a best practice among leading innovators.

The Action Method was developed taking all of these principles into account.

Breaking Projects into Primary Elements

If you know anything about magic, you know that the best tricks are the ones that are the most simple to perform. Levitation relies on pulleys, floating dollars need thread, and the disappearing coin depends on hidden pockets; all of the most remarkable tricks have the most "obvious" explanations. Similarly, the best methods for managing projects are simple and intuitive. They help you capture ideas and do something with them—no more, no less. This simple efficiency keeps you engaged and on task with as little effort as possible.

The Action Method begins with a simple premise: everything is a project. This applies not only to the big presentation on Wednesday or the new campaign you're preparing, but also to the stuff you do to advance your career (a "career development" project), or to employee development (each of your subordinates represents a single "project" in which you keep track of performance and the steps you plan to take to help him or her develop as an employee). Managing your finances is a project, as is doing your taxes or arranging the upcoming house move.

Like most creative people, I'm sure you struggle to make progress in all of your projects, with the greatest challenge being the sheer number of projects before you! But once you have everything classified as a project, you can start breaking each one down into its primary components: Action Steps, References, and Backburner Items.

Every project in life can be reduced into these three primary components. **Action Steps** are the specific, concrete tasks that inch you forward: redraft and send the memo, post the blog entry, pay the electricity bill, etc. **References** are any project-related handouts, sketches, notes, meeting minutes, manuals, Web sites, or ongoing discussions that you may want to refer back to. It is important to note that References are *not* actionable—they are simply there for reference when focusing on any particular project. Finally, there are **Backburner Items**—things that are not actionable now but may be someday. Perhaps it is an idea for a client for which there is no budget yet. Or maybe it is something you intend to do in a particular project at an unforeseen time in the future.

Let's consider a sample project for a client. Imagine a folder with that client's name on it. Inside the folder you would have a lot of References—perhaps a copy of the contract, notes from meetings, and background information on the client. The Action Steps—the stuff you need to do—could be written as a list, attached to the front of the folder. And then, perhaps on a sheet stapled to the inside back cover of the folder, your Backburner list could keep track of the nonactionable ideas that come up while working on the project—the stuff you may want to do in the future.

With this hypothetical folder in mind, you can imagine that the majority of your focus would be on the Action Steps visible on the front cover. These Action Steps are always in plain view. They catch your eye every time you glance at the project folder. And, as you review all of your project folders every day, what you're really doing is just glancing over all of the pending Action Steps.

We call it the "Action Method" because it helps us live and work with a bias toward action. The actionable aspects of every project pop out at us, and the other components are organized enough to provide peace of mind while not getting in the way of taking action.

Personal projects can also be broken down into the same three elements. If you take some time to look around your desk, you might find some notes or reminders that you've left for yourself. Perhaps you see a household bill that requires payment (an Action Step in the project "Household Management"), or a copy of your car insurance certificate (a Reference in the project "Insurance"). Maybe it is a cut-out of a great vacation spot you want to visit someday (a Backburner Item in the project "Vacation Planning").

Consider a few projects in your life—some work-related and some personal. The components of these projects are either in your head or all around you—sentences in e-mails, sketches in notebooks, and scribbles on Post-it notes. The Action Method starts by considering everything around you with a project lens and then breaking it down.

Perhaps you have an idea for a screenplay that you'd like to write someday. If so, make it a Backburner Item in the "New Screenplay Ideas" project or perhaps in a more general "Bold Ideas" project that you may review only a couple of times every year. While some projects realistically won't get much of your focus, they will help store the Backburner Items and References that you generate.

Of course, your hope is that someday a few of these Backburner Items will be converted into Action Steps—which will, in turn, lead to a new and more active project, like producing your screenplay. Action Steps are the building blocks of accomplishment. But sometimes, at certain periods of life, you can't afford to take certain actions. For this reason, it is okay to have dormant projects filled with References and Backburner Items. The time will come when some of these projects return to the surface with some Action Steps.

As you go about your day, you should think in terms of which project is associated with what you are doing at any point in time. Whether in a meeting, brainstorming session, chance conversation, article, dream, or eureka moment in the shower, you are generating Action Steps, References, and Backburner Items at a fast clip. Everything is associated with a project. Sadly, much of this output will be lost unless you capture it and assign it properly.

In the sections ahead, we will explore the three primary components of projects in more detail and how they should be managed. But the key realization should be that everything in life is a project, and every project must be broken down into Action Steps, References, and Backburner Items. It's that simple.

Of course, in the digital era, information comes to us in many forms. Projects are not always kept in folders. In fact, projects are managed across many mediums. And the components of projects come to us in the form of e-mails, status updates, files as downloads, and a barrage of links that we save daily. Nevertheless, the Action Method still applies; everything belongs to a project. With the Action Method in mind, we can make better use of online and offline tools that organize information.

The Importance of Action Steps

Action Steps are the most important components of projects—the oxygen for keeping projects alive. No Action Steps, no action, no results. The actual outcome of any idea is dependent on the Action Steps that are captured and then completed by you or delegated to someone else. Action Steps are to be revered and treated as sacred in any project.

One action-obsessed leader I met during my research was Bob Greenberg, chairman of the world-renowned digital agency R/GA, which works with clients such as Nike and Johnson & Johnson. Greenberg is admired by his colleagues and industry peers alike. Among the traits used to describe Greenberg, "productive" and "compulsive" top the list.

Greenberg has used the same morning ritual for managing his Action Steps every day since 1977. Using only certain types of pens and a certain type of notebook, Greenberg reserves time every day to process the day's Action Steps and schedule.

Greenberg shared with me that he uses two fountain pens (only

Pelikan brand fountain pens)—a larger one with blue ink and a thinner one with brown ink—to write his Action Steps, and uses a highlighter to place a series of diagonal strikes to the right of each Action Step to indicate priority. "Three marker strikes and a black dot mean most important," he explained. He also sketches his schedule for every day on the top of the page with a pencil—and then, again with a pen, he writes the names of each major pitch that R/GA is working on that day.

"I have a two-page system with multiple lists of actions," he explained. "Starting from the left-hand side, I have stuff that I can have my assistant do, then—to the right of that list—I have stuff that I need to do personally. Then to the right of that . . ."

As Greenberg continued, it became clear that he gained the most utility from the consistency and great sense of loyalty he felt for his quirky, home-brewed system.

"I believe if you don't write it down, it doesn't register," he told me. "I know it sounds painful, but it helps me know exactly what to do. I do a new version every day, I transfer the old items every morning, and I've been doing this for over thirty years." Greenberg confides that his approach is "admittedly obsessive," but it works.

The details of Greenberg's approach—the materials he uses, the symbols he assigns to each item, and the regular time at which he organizes his actions every morning—keep him engaged with his system. After all, a methodology is only effective when it is practiced consistently. While every person's system is different, the most productive people pay attention to the finer details of their rituals to keep themselves engaged. As you develop your own system to manage Action Steps, you will want to make it "sticky."

Action Steps are specific things you must do to move an idea forward. The more clear and concrete an Action Step is, the less friction you will encounter trying to do it. If an Action Step is vague or complicated, you will probably skip over it to others on your list that are more straightforward. To avoid this, start each Action Step with a verb:

> Call programmer to discuss . . .
> Install new software for . . .
> Research the possibility of . . .
> Mock up a sample of the . . .
> Update XYZ document for . . .
> Address issue of . . .

Verbs help pull us into our Action Steps at first glance, efficiently indicating what type of action is required. For similar reasons, Action Steps should be kept short.

Imagine you and I are having a conversation in a meeting. I describe to you what I want to accomplish and show you some diagrams that further describe the idea. You reply by saying, "I see what you're trying to do. There's a guy I know who designed a great Web site with the same type of functionality." Upon saying this, I record an Action Step to follow up with you regarding that Web site:

> Follow up with [your name] re: guy's Web site w/ similar functionality.

A colleague might say, "Let's revisit that old draft and consider the initial plan that we had—maybe it was better? Let me know what you think." In that case, your Action Step would be:

> Print out old draft, follow up with [colleague's name] re: alternative plan.

Sometimes you will find yourself waiting for a response to an e-mail or a phone call. It is easy to forget something when it is in someone else's court! To trigger yourself to follow up if you don't hear back, you may want to create a separate Action Step.

Action Steps arise from every idea exchange. Even the smallest of Action Steps, when captured, will make a big difference because they create momentum. A missed Action Step can cause miscommunications, more meetings, and could be the difference between success and failure in any project.

Here are some key practices:

Capture Action Steps everywhere. Ideas don't reveal themselves only in meetings, and neither should Action Steps. Ideas come up when you are reading an article, taking a shower, daydreaming, or getting ready for bed. If you think of someone that you met with a month ago regarding a certain project but have not yet followed up with, create an Action Step to "follow up with XYZ regarding..." If you are opening your mail and come across a wedding invitation, your Action Step is to RSVP.

Think of Action Steps expansively—as anything you should do (or delegate)—and capture all of them, not only the ones that arise during meetings.

Having some sort of pad or recording device handy will enable you to capture actions as they come to mind. Many people use online tools that sync with their mobile devices, such as Wunderlist, Asana, or another task management application. Whatever medium you choose to use for capturing Action Steps, it should always be readily available. Your system should also make it easy to return to your Action Steps at a later time and distinctly recall what you were thinking. And, most important, you must always be able to distinguish Action Steps from References—the regular notes and nonactionable ideas that you may have also written down.

An unowned Action Step will never be taken. Every Action Step must be owned by a single person. While some Action Steps may involve the input of different people, accountability must reside in one individual's hands at the end of the day. Some people who lead teams or have assistants will capture Action Steps and delegate them to others. However, even when the onus to complete an Action Step has been delegated to someone else, the Action Step must still be owned—and tracked—by the person ultimately responsible.

The reason comes down to accountability. The practice of simply e-mailing someone a task to complete does not provide any assurance that it will be completed. For this reason, Action Steps that you are ultimately responsible for should remain on your list until completed—even when you have delegated them to others. Simply marking that the Action Step has been delegated and to whom is sufficient:

> Print out old draft, follow up with Alex re: other plan (Oscar is doing).

Treat managerial Action Steps differently. Aside from the Action Steps that you and only you can do, there are three other types of Action Steps you should keep in mind as the leader of a project. The first type is delegated Action Steps, which we just discussed above. The second type is "Ensure Action Steps." Sometimes you will want to create an Action Step to ensure that something is completed properly in the future. Rather than being a nag to your team, you can create an Action Step that starts with the word "Ensure." For example, "Ensure that Dave updated the article with the new title." If you use a digital tool to manage your Action Steps, you can always search by the word "ensure" (to only view Action Steps that start with "ensure") and spend some time verifying that these items have been done. Creating "Ensure Action Steps" is a better alternative than sending numerous reminder e-mails to your team when you are worried about something slipping through the cracks. The last type of managerial Action Step is the "Awaiting Action Step". When you leave a voicemail for someone, send a message to a potential customer, or respond to an e-mail and clear it from your in-box, you're liable to forget to follow-up if the person fails to respond. By creating an Action Step that starts with "Awaiting," you can keep track of every ball that is out of your court. When I respond via e-mail to a potential client, I create an Action Step like "Awaiting confirmation from Joe at Apple re: consultation," saved in the project "Consulting Work." In my online task manager I will set a target date for one week later. After a week passes, I will be reminded to follow up. Sometimes I will search all my Action Steps, across projects, with the word "Awaiting" and dedicate an hour to follow up on everything.

Foster an action-oriented culture. Your team needs an action-oriented culture to capitalize on creativity. It may feel burdensome or even a bit aggressive to ask people to capture an Action Step on paper, but fostering a culture in which such reminders are welcome helps ensure that Action Steps are not lost. Some of the most productive teams I have observed are comfortable making sure that others are capturing Action Steps. Aside from friendly questioning along the lines of "Did you capture that?" some teams take a few minutes at the end of every meeting to go around the table and allow each person to recite the Action Steps that he or she captured. Doing so will almost always reveal a missed Action Step or a duplication on two people's lists. This simple practice can save time and prevent situations in which, weeks later, people are wondering who was doing what or how something got lost in the shuffle.

Attraction breeds loyalty. When it comes to the mechanics of capturing Action Steps, you should find the solution that fits you best. Keep in mind that the design of your productivity tools will affect how eager you are to use them. Attraction often breeds commitment: if you enjoy your method for staying organized, you are more likely to use it consistently over time. For this reason, little details like the colors of folders you use or the quality of the paper can actually help boost your productivity.

In her book *The Substance of Style*, journalist Virginia Postrel shares an anecdote about usability guru Donald Norman's assertion that "attractive things work better." When the first color computer monitors became available commercially, Norman wanted to justify the value of buying the expensive monitors instead of the standard black-and-white displays. Nowadays, this decision might seem obvious, but back in the day before the World Wide Web and color printers, the value of a color monitor for functions like word processing was unproven. "I got myself a color display and took it home for a week," Norman recalled. "When the week was over, I had two findings. The first finding was that I was right, there was absolutely no advantage to color. The second was that I was not going to give it up." In her analysis of Norman's findings, Postrel explains, "The difference lay not in 'information processing' but in 'affect,' in how full-color monitors made people feel about their work."

In other words, the aesthetics of the tools you use to make ideas happen matter.

Maintaining a Backburner

During brainstorming, in the midst of working on a project, or during a long night's drive, you're likely to conceive ideas that may not be actionable yet. For instance, you might think of some things you would do in a current project if only you had more time or a bigger budget. Or you might come up with vague ideas for new projects to consider in the future. Either way, you are liable to forget these ideas if you fail to capture them and develop a ritual for returning to them over time.

You won't want to record these thoughts as Action Steps because they are not yet actionable. And writing them down among your other Reference notes is not sufficient because you are unlikely to read old project References in the future. We call these ideas "Backburner Items"—stuff that isn't actionable yet but may be someday (and is worthy of revisiting periodically).

Sometimes these fledgling ideas are the best ones. Rumor has it that the melody of the hit song "Sweet Baby James" popped into songwriter James Taylor's head during a long drive from New England to the Carolinas. For just such occasions, Taylor carried around a microrecorder that he used to capture little melodies or ideas he wanted to revisit. While driving, he reached for the recorder and quickly recited to himself the concept and melody—along with a note to toy with the song idea. It was apparently not until much later, when he listened to his recorded thoughts, that he wrote the song.

We are humans, not machines. With our creativity comes the tendency to think of random ideas and actions we might want to take but not right at that time. Idea generation is often tangential to the active projects in our lives. But the fact that the timing is off does not mean that the thought isn't worthy of future consideration.

The Backburner keeps your ideas—and the possible future actions you might take to make the ideas happen—alive. It is critical to making an impact with your creativity because, most often, great ideas that are not yet actionable are quickly forgotten.

Set up your Backburner. Functionally, the Backburner is easy to employ. Set aside an area at the bottom or side of your notes—or perhaps a separate page—to capture Backburner Items that come up. As you aggregate Backburner Items over the course of a day, you will want to use a central repository for storage. They can be assigned to a current project name (a particular client, for example), or to a more general Backburner folder reserved for distant ideas like a book you may want to write or a business you'd like to start.

I've seen a number of people draw a box on the bottom of every note page. They fill it with Backburner Items over the course of a meeting, and then, at the end of the day, place the Backburner Items into some sort of folder or running text document on their computer.

Create a Backburner ritual. Of course, putting stuff in your Backburner is not enough. You need to periodically revisit and curate the Backburner as time goes on. Make it a habit. One agency creative director I interviewed keeps his Backburner as a running Microsoft Word document on his computer. On the last Sunday of every month, he prints out this ten- or fifteen-page document and, pen in one hand and beer in the other, spends half an hour editing the list. As he reviews each entry, he either cuts it, keeps it, or—in some cases—turns the Backburner Item into a series of Action Steps.

Consider making a recurring monthly "Backburner Review" appointment in your calendar. Ritualize the time you spend revisiting the half-baked ideas that may someday transform your work or life. It is easy to forget your Backburner (and, most of the time, you should!), but you need to stoke it from time to time.

When you review your Backburner, you will find that some of the items have suddenly become realistic, actionable goals, while others have gradually become irrelevant. Sometimes a long-held Backburner Item is actually the solution to a new problem you face.

References Are Worth Storing, Not Revering

The third and final component of every project is "References." The tendency to take notes, make sketches, and compulsively save various types of handouts and reference materials is ingrained from our early days in elementary school. We were trained to write down everything we learned, relevant or not, and we often memorized everything we'd written for the big exam day.

For many of us, this habit of recording and organizing everything has become a time- and space-consuming behavior with no real payoff. We take notes in meetings, we watch these notes accumulate in a pile on our desks along with other handouts and articles for reference, and then we eventually take the time to "file" them in some sort of elaborate system. To what end?

Two of the greatest benefits of storing References with some sense of organization are simply the reduction of clutter and the peace of mind—even if we seldom refer back to them. Microsoft Research scientist Gordon Bell famously took Reference management to the extreme when he decided to log his entire life's personal data—every e-mail, every phone conversation, every day's face-to-face conversations (using a head-mounted video camera), and even his health-related data (via a heart-rate monitor).

The recording of this data happened automatically, allowing Bell to proceed with his life knowing that everything was being documented. His experiment concluded with a massive archive of the Reference items of his life. His struggle, which he shares in his book *Total Recall*, was making sense of it all. One of the greatest benefits discovered by Bell was the liberation of his "meat-based memory," allowing him to engage in more creativity and actionable stuff. By letting go of the static stuff that typically burdened his mind—and piled up around him—he became more productive. But the question remains for those of us who don't have head-mounted video cameras and therefore must record and organize information manually: How much energy should we invest in capturing and organizing References?

It turns out that most of us seldom refer back to all of this static documentation that clutters our lives. While we might cherish the opportunity to refer back to the thoughts or main points gathered in meetings and brainstorms of the past, we rarely have the luxury to do so. Truth be told, we can barely complete our Action Steps amidst the chaos of the everyday, let alone refer back to References.

You must find ways, using modern technology if possible, to manage the References of your projects without compromising the precious energy you have for what is actionable.

References obstruct your bias toward action. It is common that Action Steps get lost in the shuffle of nonactionable stuff. The more energy you spend on scribbling down notes, the more liable you are to miss the opportunity to capture valuable Action Steps. Even if you do manage to write the Action Steps down, they often become obscured amidst sketches, thoughts, and other notes. The notebook closes and—hours later—the Action Steps disappear from your mind along with the potential they hold.

Even with a well-organized system for managing References, you might consider reducing your scribe-like tendencies.

Use a chronological pile (or file). I have observed some people who abandon project files and intricate Reference management systems in favor of keeping a single chronological pile of all notes or handouts from all meetings—across all projects. In the age of online scheduling applications and software, it is easier than ever before to match meetings in the past with exact dates. Simply place your notes from every meeting (regardless of project) at the top of a Reference pile immediately after each meeting. Every month, place this pile into a date-labeled file folder. With the help of your datebook, you should be able to easily jump back to the notes and other References related to any meeting you attended in the past. This is an efficient and simple way to find notes for particular projects. It requires no time to file and sort, and keeps the rest of your space clear of dusty archival materials.

Feel the flow of References. You have an article, Web site, or note that might be valuable later on. Taking the following steps will make the Reference easily accessible when you need it.

Question it. "What is the relevance? For what purpose would I refer back to this at some point?" If you can't answer this question, throw the Reference out! Some people claim they must write things down to learn and understand concepts. This is fine, but consider discarding the notes and saving only the Action Steps. However, what if the item is important and must be saved for later on?

Label it. Ask yourself, "How should I identify this Reference so I can intuitively find it later?" If you keep a chronological file, the label need only be the date. Otherwise, consider what project name is most appropriate.

File it. If you're using a paper-based system, place the Reference in the appropriate folder (or pile, if you are taking a chronological approach paired with your calendar). There are many great software and online applications that we have seen used across industries. For example, Evernote (evernote.com) is a Web-based application that allows users to take snapshots or record quick text or voice messages and then store them by a label (project name). Other online document applications from Google, Apple, and others can also be used to store References organized by project.

Practicing the Action Method

The Action Method reduces project management to its most basic elements so that you can focus your energy on the important stuff, like actually completing tasks and making progress. The best way to get started is to look at a few of your current projects through the Action Method lens. Try to see each project as a collection of the three elements: Action Steps, Backburner Items, and References.

Take a moment to consider two "projects" in your life right now: a personal project related to your family or home, and a work project. Think about the current Action Steps for each of these projects—the stuff that you need to do. Are these Action Steps dispersed throughout messages sitting in your e-mail in-box? A notebook or journal? Sketched on a napkin?

Do you have any Backburner Items for these projects? What about References? Are they stacked around your office, or tucked away in files where you'll never find them?

Here are a few things to keep in mind:

Actions Steps should be managed separate from e-mail. Have you ever found yourself rereading e-mails repeatedly, trying to distill the Action Steps when the time comes to actually do them? E-mail can kill productivity because the actionable information you receive is always clouded by Reference material. Your Action Steps become hidden within the e-mails and then gradually buried by other e-mails. For this reason, Action Steps should have a space (or system) of their own. We will discuss how to pair e-mail with a system for managing Action Steps in the section ahead.

When it comes to taking action, work and personal life collide (and that's okay). People tend to separate the actions they must take in their personal lives from those in their professional lives. While formal "to-do" lists and applications empower you at work, Post-it notes on your refrigerator keep you on task at home. But observing the most productive people reveals that Action Steps are Action Steps, regardless of their context. Priorities may change, but managing everything actionable in one system is your best bet. New online task management tools with mobile versions help make your life's Action Steps accessible to you wherever you are. By using the same system, you are able to prioritize (and complete) Action Steps whenever (and wherever) you want. You will also find that you and your team are more likely to complete work-related Action Steps when they are intermingled with personal Action Steps.

Actions are truly "delegated" only when they are accepted. While many project management methods support "to-do" lists that multiple people can share, true accountability is never achieved unless your team members choose to accept their delegated Action Steps. Not only should outstanding work tasks be transparent to all members of the team (or at least one or two other colleagues), but your colleagues should actively accept or reject Action Steps that you assign them. This conceptual "handshake" creates accountability and eliminates the ambiguous Action Steps that notoriously clog the progress in any project.

Teams that exchange Action Steps via e-mail can agree that some form of acceptance or confirmation is required. When a colleague sends you an Action Step that is unclear or incorrect, you should reject it and seek more clarification. Doing so will prevent the Action Step from lingering in the realm of ambiguity. For teams that use paper lists or wall charts, a best practice is to have all members write up their own Action Steps (in their own handwriting)—even those that are delegated to them. Doing so implies understanding and acceptance. Regardless of your method for managing Action

Steps, it is vital that you (and your project partners) never accept an Action Step unless it is clear and able to be executed.

Sequential tasking is better than multitasking. It is impossible to complete two Action Steps at once, which would suggest that "multitasking" is a myth. However, you can easily focus on more than one project at once if the Action Steps in all of your projects are defined and organized. You should aim to jump quickly between projects with as little unproductive downtime as possible. The secret is fully breaking down the elements of each project.

Capture and Make Time for Processing

As you move through your day of meetings, brainstorms, and other occasions of creativity, you will start to accumulate Action Steps, References, and Backburner Items. Handouts, random pages of notes, e-mails, and social network messages will build up all around you. Often these items will get buried in notebooks, pockets, online in-boxes, and computer files almost as soon as they are created or received.

Ideally, in your written notes you will have kept your Action Steps separate from everything else. However, you will still need time for processing—going through all of your day's notes and communications and distilling them down to the primary elements. For those who still take paper notes and appreciate tangible project management, you will want to use a tangible in-box—a general pile of stuff that has yet to be classified. Most productivity frameworks—like David Allen's *Getting Things Done*—suggest such a central clearinghouse for all of the stuff that you accumulate but can't immediately execute or file. This in-box is not a final destination, but rather a transit terminal where items await processing. During a busy day of meetings, you will not have time to start taking action or filing things away.

How about all of the digital stuff that flows in every day? Your e-mail in-box is the primary landing spot, but information also flows into other online applications. While your tangible in-box, sitting on your desk, is singular, the digital equivalent is becoming more of a collective. Ideally, you should set your settings in social networks to forward messages to your e-mail in-box for the sake of aggregation. When you commit time for processing, you'll want to limit the number of places you need to visit. If you can't aggregate the flow of e-mails and other digital communications in the same place, then you need to define the various pieces of your collective digital in-box. For example, my collective digital in-box includes my e-mail program (which receives messages from all other networks), a Twitter aggregator, and the in-box in my task management application (where I accept/reject stuff sent from my colleagues who use the same application—and then manage this information by project). When the time comes for processing, these are the three digital places I need to visit, along with the tangible in-box full of papers on my desk.

As you can see, the "in-box" of the twenty-first century varies for everyone. You must concretely define your collective in-box before you start processing. Peace of mind and productivity starts when you know where everything is. The combined in-box says, "Don't worry, all of your stuff (and the Action Steps, Backburner Items, and References contained within) are in a defined place, waiting for you and ready to be sorted."

If you live a digital lifestyle, your ability to process your in-box may be at particular risk without some sense of discipline. The reason: in the era of mobile devices and constant connectivity, it has become all too easy for others to send us messages. As such, our ability to control our focus is often crippled by the never-ending flow of incoming phone calls, e-mails, text messages, and in-person interruptions—not to mention messages from other online services. Thus it is important that you avoid the trap of what I have come to call "reactionary work flow."

The state of reactionary work flow occurs when you get stuck simply reacting to whatever flows into the top of an in-box. Instead of focusing on what is most important and actionable, you spend too much time just trying to stay afloat. Reactionary work flow prevents you from being more proactive with your energy. The act of processing requires discipline and imposing some blockades around your focus. For this reason, many leaders perform their processing at night or at a time when the flow dies down.

Time spent processing is arguably the most valuable and productive time of your day. While processing, you will sort everything and distinguish Action Steps, Backburner Items, and References. With Action Steps, you will decide what can be done quickly and what must be tracked over time by project—and possibly delegated. With other materials, you will make judgments about what can be thrown away and what must be filed.

As you start to tackle your collective in-box, you will realize that any in-box, on its own, is a pretty bad action management tool. It is difficult to keep your Action Steps separate from References and other noise. The constant stream of e-mail certainly doesn't help. In addition to e-mail, you may also receive other types of incoming communications in the form of Tweets, Facebook messages, etc. Some are actionable, or contain actionable elements, while others are simply for reference (or for fun).

Given the unyielding flow of communications, you will want to capture and manage your Action Steps separately. Despite the many tricks involving "action subfolders" and other ways to manage and prioritize Action Steps within an e-mail system, there is nothing better than giving Action Steps their own sacred space to be managed by project. The Action Method suggests that Action Steps should be managed separately from communications. The solution can be as simple as a spreadsheet or to-do list where all Action Steps are tracked (and can be sorted by project name or due date). You can also make use of more advanced project management applications that manage Action Steps and support delegation and collaboration. What you want to avoid is a mishmash of actionable items amidst hundreds of verbose e-mails and other messages scattered in various places.

For teams that manage Action Steps via e-mail, actionable e-mails should have "Action" as the first word in the subject line. For Reference e-mails, you should start the e-mail's subject line with "FYI." By establishing a common language with your colleagues, everyone will be able to sort their e-mail in-box and view Action Steps using these keywords.

Feel the flow of the Action Method. Every new day generates more ideas, notes, and communications that flow into your collective in-box. At periods of the day that you designate for processing, you break everything down into Action Steps, Backburner Items, and References. You associate each item with a project, whether it is personal or work-related. As you are doing this, quick actions are being completed while longer-term Action Steps are being added to the appropriate project's task list or your task management application—with a project name (and due date if necessary). Backburner Items are added to the appropriate folder or list. And Reference materials are either being discarded or stored by project or perhaps in a chronological file.

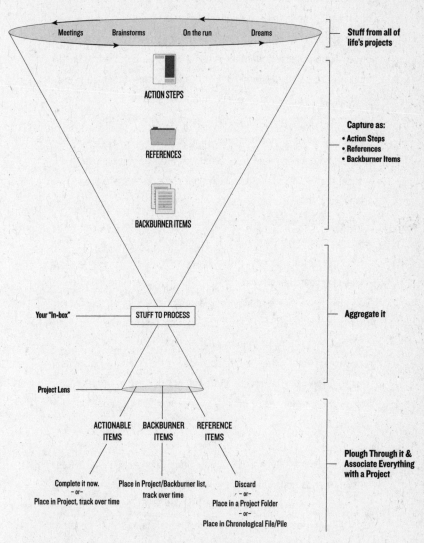

Stuff from all of
life's projects

Capture as:
• Action Steps
• References
• Backburner Items

Aggregate it

Plough Through it &
Associate Everything
with a Project

Meetings   Brainstorms   On the run   Dreams

ACTION STEPS

REFERENCES

BACKBURNER ITEMS

Your "In-box" —— STUFF TO PROCESS

Project Lens

ACTIONABLE
ITEMS

BACKBURNER
ITEMS

REFERENCE
ITEMS

Complete it now.
– or –
Place in Project, track over time

Place in Project/Backburner list,
track over time

Discard
– or –
Place in a Project Folder
– or –
Place in Chronological File/Pile

Feel the flow, from creativity to capturing the elements, processing them, and then managing them
by project.

Capture! Capture Action Steps relentlessly. During a brainstorm or a meeting, or on the run, you will generate ideas, and those ideas will disappear unless they are broken down into concrete verb-driven Action Steps. Collect them using whatever notebook or technology option you desire—but try to keep Action Steps separate so they stand out amidst your References and Backburner Items. Some people e-mail themselves throughout the day, while others capture tasks on a mobile device that automatically syncs with an online task management tool. Whatever method you choose, it is critical that your Action Steps stand out and can be managed separately from all of the other stuff.

If you find yourself with extraneous scraps of paper or unfiled e-mails containing Action Steps, Backburner Items, and References, place them in your in-box for processing.

Identify your collective in-box. In addition to your physical in-box, you also have your e-mail in-box among other digital sources of information. Identify and then consolidate the number of digital in-boxes that you need to manage.

Process! Take a few hours each day (or a minimum of a few nights per week) to process the contents of your in-box. As you review the pile (or list of e-mails), discern what is actionable and what is not.

- If actionable, identify the Action Steps. For Action Steps that can be accomplished quickly (like make a short phone call or pay a bill), do them right away. David Allen calls this the "two-minute rule"—if it can be done in under two minutes, it should be done right away. After all, it will take a minute or so just to enter it into your system, so why not just take care of it already?
- Whatever action management system you use, Action Steps

should be recorded in a consistent way, assigned to a project, and given a due date (when applicable). By doing this, you are setting yourself up for ultimate productivity.

- Place Backburner Items in your Backburner folder, labeled with the appropriate project name.

- Try to discard as many References as you can, because most handouts and notes will ultimately never be used. For those References that must be stored, file them away by project or use the chronological pile approach.

PRIORITIZATION:
Managing Your Energy
Across Life's Projects

DYNAMIC CREATIVE PROJECTS—as well as cumbersome logistical projects—become more manageable when they are broken down into elements. Once we are able to approach our work (and life) as a series of Action Steps, Backburner Items, and References, we will have to decide where to start. We must prioritize because we can only focus on one Action Step at a time. Prioritization should help us maintain both incremental progress as well as momentum for our long-term objectives. Prioritization is a force that relies on sound judgment, self-discipline, and some helpful pressure from others.

Keep an Eye on Your Energy Line

I spent one afternoon a while back with Max Schorr, the publisher of *GOOD*, a monthly magazine focused on doing good, and his team.

A group of true idealists, the staff found themselves constantly overburdened and overextended—striving to do everything while also striving for perfection. As Schorr put it, "At *GOOD* we hate to waste anything, and given our surplus of idea generation, the one thing we waste tons of is energy."

If you have lots of ideas, you probably have the tendency to get involved with or start lots of projects. Projects can require tremendous amounts of mental energy, from capturing and organizing the elements to actually applying your creative talents to solve problems and complete Action Steps. Energy is your most precious commodity. Regardless of who you are, you have only a finite amount of it. Just as a computer's operating capacity is limited to the amount of memory (or RAM) installed, we all have our limits.

As you decide where to focus your precious energy, visualize all of your projects along a spectrum that starts at "Extreme" and goes all the way down to "Idle." How much energy should your current projects receive?

EXTREME	HIGH	MEDIUM	LOW	IDLE
Version 2.0	AMO Sales Page	Team Blog	Financial Management	Screenplay
		Book Proposal	Office Renovation	Graph 1.0
			Map Redesign	

Place your projects along an energy line according to how much energy they should receive.

At any given point in time there may be a couple of projects that you should be extremely focused on, while others may be semi-important or perhaps idle for the time being. If you were to place projects along the spectrum, the extremely important projects would be placed on the "Extreme" end of the spectrum and the others would be placed accordingly farther down toward "Idle." Keep in mind that you are *not* placing your projects along the spectrum based on how much time you are spending on them. Rather, you are placing your projects according to how much energy they should receive based on their importance.

A project placed at the "Extreme" end of the energy line should be the most important for the time being—worthy of the majority of your energy. Projects should be placed according to their economic and strategic value. The concept of the Energy Line is meant to address our tendency to spend a lot of time on projects that are interesting but perhaps not important enough to warrant such an investment of energy.

Viewing your projects along an Energy Line prompts certain questions: How much of your time are you spending on what? Are you focused on the right things?

Amidst the everyday craziness of a creative enterprise, it is hard to keep track of energy and where it's being used. The Energy Line is a simple mechanism to help us measure and adjust a team's energy allocation. We have seen many people use similar concepts to help themselves visualize the projects in their lives according to priority. After considering your Energy Line for just a few minutes, you can get a sense of whether your energy for that week, day, or even that hour is being managed properly.

The Energy Line exercise is also a helpful way for teams to agree on prioritization. Some teams will gather around a corkboard or whiteboard and, together, write the names of all of their major projects on small cards. The team will then place the cards along the Energy Line according to their importance and how much collective focus each project should get from the team. At first, you may find that too many projects are being placed near the "Extreme" zone of the spectrum. This is a natural tendency because each project solicits different levels of interest from different members of the team. Such disagreements are great because they help the team prioritize collectively.

As you consider your Energy Line, you will want to make the tough decisions about what projects need to live on low energy for a while. Whether or not you use the Energy Line exercise, all teams should discuss and debate how their energy is allocated. Energy is a finite resource that is seldom managed well.

If every Action Step belongs to a project and you have your projects spread across a spectrum of how you wish to allocate your energy—then you will have clear direction on which Action Steps you should do first and how you should budget your time.

Reconciling Urgent vs. Important

While the Energy Line perspective can help us allocate our energy across projects, we are still bound to drift off course as soon as unexpected and urgent items arise. When something is urgent, we rush to do it. Even if it can wait—or is someone else's job—our tendency is to hoard urgent items because they always seem more pressing than stuff associated with longer-term projects. As leaders of creative projects, we feel an impulse to solve everything quickly. I call this "Creator's Immediacy"—an instinct to take care of every problem and operational task, no matter how large or small, as soon as it comes up, similar to a mother's instinct for the care of a newborn baby. However, it becomes nearly impossible to pursue long-term goals when you are guided solely by the most recent e-mail in your in-box or call from a client.

Fortunately, there are ways to manage the urgent stuff without compromising progress on long-term projects. The capacity to do so starts with compartmentalization, shared values, and the power of clarity.

If you've ever used Priceline.com, an ATM, or a cell phone, then you've used technology developed and patented by Walker Digital. Primarily a research and development outfit, this seventy-person company has developed and successfully patented a variety of ideas across technological industries. As an intensely creative company, the Walker Digital team is constantly developing new ideas and is liable to suffer from Creator's Immediacy. Nevertheless, the company's leadership takes pride in its ability to operate efficiently on a daily basis while also innovating with the future in mind.

At any given moment, half the company is dreaming up new ideas while the other half is managing and licensing the patented ones. In such an environment, one might expect the urgent operational needs of the business to quickly compromise the energy allocated to multiyear research projects. But they don't. Walker Digital's track record suggests that it has been able to maintain a focus on long-term projects despite the growing operational demands.

President Jon Ellenthal admits how difficult it is to develop new ideas and operate a business at the same time. "Development and operations are fundamentally different burdens," Ellenthal explained to me. "The gravitational pull over an operator is nearly impossible to escape. When faced with a choice of what to do next, what must be done today will always trump what might be developed for tomorrow." In other words, there is a great tension between the urgent operational items with current projects that arise every day and the more important (but less timely) items that are liable to be perpetually postponed. Without some sense of discipline, the company would drown in the everyday "urgent items" to the detriment of the company's success over time.

Walker Digital's distinctive culture may help explain its ability to consistently focus on long-term projects. For starters, the company is privately owned. "No normal investor would ever have the patience for turning ideas into patents," explains Ellenthal. The time and expense invested in the patent side of the business might scare away ordinary investors, but for the Walker Digital employees, it has only reinforced the value of ideas. "The amount of energy we invest in turning ideas into commercial assets encourages people to maintain their ideas—and keep them top of mind. . . . Everyone knows how valuable an idea may become for us."

A shared respect for the potential of ideas empowers people to speak up when day-to-day operations start to interfere. Ellenthal and his executive team take particular pride in the company's straightforwardness. His colleague and chief marketing officer, Shirley Bergin, elaborated: "Our value for clarity overcomes the risk and fear of speaking up when something doesn't make sense." For a company that is entrenched in both operations and long-term innovation simultaneously, the aspiration for clarity maintains a constant, healthy debate around energy allocation.

Walker Digital's shared value for ideas—and a culture that constantly seeks clarity—empowers people to quarantine themselves for extended periods of time while researching long-term projects. The company is even structured to allow half the company to engage in long-term pursuits while the other half oversees the legal and operational side of managing the patents. Through a finely tuned culture, Walker Digital is able to keep long-term pursuits alive.

Whether you work alone or within a team (or company) full of people, the first step is to discern what is urgent versus what is important in the long term. Especially in the creative environment, important projects often require substantive time and mental loyalty. The constant flow of "urgent" matters that arise for you—the daily questions from clients, the bills to pay, the problems and glitches—threaten to interfere with your long-term objectives. The challenge is compounded for projects that you created yourself. As the creator, you feel a sense of ownership and, with it, a heavy impulse to address every task or problem immediately.

There is too much focus on "fixing." How can you maintain long-term objectives rather than suffer at the mercy of urgent tasks? It is called prioritization. And to prioritize, you must become more disciplined and use methods that prompt compartmentalization and focus.

Here are some tips to consider:

Keep two lists. When it comes to organizing your Action Steps of the day—and how your energy will be allocated—create two lists: one for urgent items and another for important ones. Long-term goals and priorities deserve a list of their own and should not compete against the urgent items that can easily consume your day. Once you have two lists, you can preserve different periods of time to focus on each.

Choose five projects that matter most. Recognize that compromise is a necessity. Some people narrow their list of important items to just five specific things. Family is often one of the five, along with a few other specific projects or passions that require everyday attention. The most important aspect of this list is what's *not* on it. When urgent matters come up, the "important" stuff you are working on that didn't make your list should be dropped. You may be surprised to see how much energy you spend on off-list items!

Make a daily "focus area." About ten months after launching our team's own online productivity application, Action Method Online, a colleague suggested to me that we create a special "focus area" within the application to which you could drag up to five Action Steps—from any project—that you wanted to focus on today. This arrangement suggested that, regardless of whatever else cropped up that day, the focus area had to be cleared before you went to sleep at night. Keeping your focus list short makes it easier to constantly review throughout the day—to ensure that you focus on the more important items.

Don't dwell. When urgent matters arise, they tend to evoke anxiety. We dwell on the potential negative outcomes of all the challenges before us—even after action is taken. Worrying wastes time and distracts us from returning to the important stuff. When it comes to addressing urgent items, break them down into Action Steps and challenge yourself to reallocate your energy as soon as the Action Steps are completed.

It is also helpful to consider whether or not certain concerns are within or beyond our influence. Often our worries are for the unknown and there is nothing more we can do to influence the outcome. Once you have taken action to resolve a problem, recognize that the outcome is no longer under your influence.

Don't hoard urgent items. Even when you delegate operational responsibilities to someone else, you may still find yourself hoarding urgent items as they arise. When you care so deeply about a project, you'll want to resolve things yourself. Say an e-mail arrives from a client with a routine problem. Even though the responsibility may lie with someone else on your team, you might think, "Oh, this is really a quick fix; I'll just take care of it." And gradually your energy will start to shift away from long-term pursuits. Hoarding urgent items is one of the most damaging tendencies I've noticed in creative professionals who have encountered early success. When you are in the position to do so, challenge yourself to delegate urgent items.

Create a Responsibility Grid. If you have a partner, you'll want to divide and conquer various tasks for efficiency. Some teams create a "Responsibility Grid" to help them compartmentalize. This is also a tool that I used with co-heads of teams while working at Goldman Sachs. Across the top of the chart (the horizontal x-axis) you write the names of the people on the team. Then, down the left side of the page (the vertical y-axis), you write all of the common issues that come up in a typical week. Place a check in the grid for which team member (listed along the top) is responsible for which type of issue (along the side).

For example, if you're a small application-development team, your list of issues might include "inquiry for a sale or team discount," "bug report from a user," "report of lost data," and "suggestion for a new feature." As a team, you go through each person's column and check the issues he or she is responsible for. Once completed and agreed upon, this chart sends an important message about who is (and, more important, who is not) allowed to respond to certain issues. The exercise in itself will help quench everyone's impulse to do everything themselves and will streamline your team's operations.

RESPONSIBILITY GRID: Who gets involved with what?

Issue or Circumstance	Brittany	Alex	Scott
Client needs to discuss or get new copy of bill	✓		
User reports copyright or spam-related violation	✓		
User reports repeated (third/forth) copyright violations	✓		✓
Top 500 company inquires about product integration		✓	✓

Use a Responsibility Grid to decide who does or does not need to get involved with whatever comes up.

Create windows of nonstimulation. To achieve long-term goals in the age of always-on technology and free-flowing communication, create windows of time dedicated to uninterrupted project focus. Merlin Mann, founder of the productivity Web site 43folders.com, has called for the need to "make time to make." It is no surprise that Mann is also known for begging people *not* to e-mail him (in fact, he refuses to answer any suggestions or requests via e-mail). After years of writing about productivity and life hacks, Mann realized that the level of interruption increases in direct proportion to one's level of availability.

Many people I have interviewed preserve blocks of time during their day—often late nights and early mornings—as precious opportunities to make progress on important items with little risk of urgent matters popping up. For Mac users, there is a standard desktop feature called "Spaces" that allows you to change your desktop view to show only certain applications at a time. One standard practice I have seen in the field is keeping e-mail and all other communication applications in a single Space—and then, when writing or working on a project, keeping that application in a different Space. If you don't use Apple's Spaces feature, you can simply minimize (or quit) all communication applications during certain periods of your day.

Of course, this practice requires great discipline and the ability to extract yourself from reactionary work flow—the state of always responding to what comes in to us. However, through windows of nonstimulation, you will reclaim the power to focus on what you believe is most important.

Darwinian Prioritization

Of course, we are not always equipped to manage our energy and determine urgent versus important on our own. Despite our attempts to compartmentalize, emotion and anxiety are likely to interfere with our judgment as we seek to prioritize actions and decisions.

Those around us—our colleagues, clients, friends, and family—can add a positive natural force for prioritization if we are willing to channel it. I call this "Darwinian Prioritization" because it works through natural selection: the more we hear about things, the more likely we are to focus on them. Another less glamorous term for this process is "nagging."

Many teams rely on the natural force of nagging and peer pressure to better prioritize and allocate energy across projects. One such company is a New York–based creative agency called Brooklyn Brothers. The agency's senior partners, Guy Barnett and Stephen Rutterford, manage a small but particularly prolific team that churns out work for clients as well as in-house entrepreneurial ventures that range from chocolate bars to children's books.

"We have lots of ideas . . . we are a factory of ideas . . . but we develop less than 10 percent of them," Rutterford explained to me. After asking a battery of questions about their project management tools and creative process, I was surprised to learn that they were very hands-off with their team. Rather than use advanced project management systems, the team calls meetings only when needed (rather than having regularly scheduled check-ins). At one point during our discussion, Barnett leaned forward and explained, "Our secret in execution around here is really quite simple: nagging." He went on: "We repeat stuff like robots a thousand times. . . . A best practice for us is to use nagging tempered by humor; we sit around a table and feel responsible to each other. . . . If you're annoying, people will do things because they'll want you to shut up!" At Brooklyn Brothers, the open office-seating structure makes it even easier for people to stand up and quickly remind (nag) one another about an impending deadline or upcoming meeting. This may sound like a chaotic way for a team to prioritize and manage its energy, but a surprising number of highly productive teams swear by it.

I've noticed that nagging as a positive force for prioritization works across other industries as well. Roger Berkowitz, CEO of Legal Sea Foods—a $215-million company with over four thousand employees—explained in an interview with *Inc.* magazine how his work style depends on the forces of nagging. "People who want me to do something . . . have to remind me repeatedly," he explained. "It's management by being nagged."

The reliance on—and even the encouragement of—nagging may at first appear bothersome. It may be annoying to be constantly reminded about something while trying to immerse yourself in a creative project. However, amidst the chaos of meetings and trying to prioritize the elements of multiple projects, nagging from others helps you prioritize by natural selection. When someone is consistently bothering you about something, chances are you have become a bottleneck in the team's productivity. As you allocate your energy across projects, it is often difficult to know how your decisions affect others. Certain Action Steps on your list may become more important than others due to popular demand. Nagging is a force that can boost productivity through collective prioritization—as long as the culture supports it.

EXECUTION:
Always Moving the Ball Forward

Genius is 1 percent inspiration and 99 percent perspiration.

—Thomas Edison

THOMAS EDISON'S FAMOUS quote rings especially true in the world of innovation. Execution, of course, is predominantly perspiration. Organizing each project's elements, scheduling time, allocating energy, and then relentlessly completing Action Steps comprises the lion's share of pushing ideas to fruition.

Yet, as we move further along the trajectory of execution, we are liable to get lost in the "project plateau." We know we're on the plateau when we are overwhelmed with Action Steps and can see no end in sight. Our energy and commitment—and thus a willingness to tolerate the sometimes painful process of execution—are naturally high only when an idea is first conceived. The honeymoon period quickly fades as Action Steps pile up and compete with our other ongoing commitments. Our ideas become less interesting as we realize the implied responsibilities and sheer amount of work required to execute them.

The easiest and most seductive escape from the project plateau is the most dangerous one: a new idea. New ideas offer a quick return to the high energy and commitment zone, but they also cause us to lose focus. As the new star rises, our execution efforts for the original idea start to fall off. The end result? A plateau filled with the skeletons of abandoned ideas. Although it is part of the creative's essence to constantly generate new ideas, our addiction to new ideas is also what often cuts our journeys short.

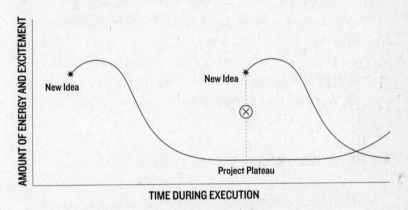

Avoid the tendency to escape the lulls of the project plateau by developing new ideas.

To push your ideas to fruition, you must develop the capacity to endure, and even thrive, as you traverse the project plateau. You must reconsider the way you approach execution. The forces you can use to sustain your focus and renew your energy do not come naturally. Making ideas actually happen boils down to self-discipline and the ways in which you take action.

By proposing the Action Method as the most effective way to approach projects, I've already made the argument that you should navigate life with a bias toward action. But why do we so often struggle to actually take action?

There are many reasons for procrastination. Aside from the desire to generate more ideas rather than take action on existing ones, another factor that discourages action is fear. We have a fear of rejection or premature judgment. Many novelists and other artists admit that they are sitting on half-baked projects that have not been shared with anyone because they're "just not ready yet." But what if one never really feels ready?

Sometimes, to delay action even longer, we resort to bureaucracy. Bureaucracy was born out of the human desire for complete assurance before taking action. When we don't want to take action, we find reasons to wait. We use "waiting" nicknames like "awaiting approval," "following procedures," "further research," or "consensus building." However, even when the next step is unclear, the best way to figure it out is to take some incremental action. Constant motion is the key to execution.

Act Without Conviction

> The truth is, creativity isn't about wild talent as much as it's about productivity. To find a few ideas that work, you need to try a lot that don't. It's a pure numbers game.
>
> —Robert Sutton, professor of management science and engineering,
> Stanford School of Engineering

The notion of taking rapid action without conviction defies the conventional wisdom to think before you act. But for the creative mind, the cost of waiting for conviction can be too great to bear. Waiting builds apathy and increases the likelihood that another idea will capture our fancy and energy. What's more, if you were to build lots of conviction after much analysis, it might leave you too deeply committed to a single plan of action and unable to change course when necessary.

Traditional practices such as writing a business plan—ultimately a static document that will inevitably be changed on the fly as unforeseen opportunities arise—must be weighed against the benefits of just starting to take incremental action on your idea, even if such early actions feel reckless. Taking action helps expose whether we are on the right or wrong path more quickly and more definitively than pure contemplation ever could.

During one of my visits to IDEO, a world-renowned product innovation and design consultancy, I had the opportunity to spend a morning with Sam Truslow, a senior team member who oversees the company's work with organizations like Hewlett-Packard. Like many folks at IDEO, Truslow readily admits that the famed "idea factory" is widely misunderstood. "What makes us tick is not just having good ideas, despite what clients think," says Truslow. "When people want new ideas, what they are really saying is that they can't execute." What IDEO does provide is an incredibly effective structure for the execution of ideas—often ideas that their clients may have already had. For Truslow, IDEO's tendency to constantly "make stuff" throughout the creative process is perhaps the most critical ingredient to the company's success.

In the process of idea generation in most environments, promising leads become diluted through debate or are simply skipped over during the natural progression of discussion. When a group decides to act upon an idea—whether this idea requires initial research or some sort of preliminary design or mock-up—the team will often strive for consensus before even discussing execution. This search for consensus stalls real progress.

IDEO's common practices for idea implementation more closely resemble a curious four-year-old experimenting with LEGOs than a well-established corporate design and business development firm. When team members have an idea for how something might look or function, they'll simply have a prototype built and start tinkering—

despite what stage of the design process they are in. IDEO's rapid prototyping practices are part of a clever strategy to overcome some of the biggest boundaries to making ideas happen.

Team members at IDEO rapidly pursue ideas even during the preliminary phases of a project. They are able to do so using a unique set of resources that empower employees to take rapid action on the fledgling ideas that arise during brainstorming. For starters, all designers have access to "The Shop"—a multimillion-dollar fully staffed department within the company that has the latest tools to rapidly create mock-ups out of metal, wood, or plastic. A quick tour of The Shop provides a tangible, visual history of the development of landmark projects like the standard mouse for Microsoft with a scroll wheel and the Palm V design for 3Com.

Truslow explained to me that there is less need for consensus in a team when individuals are empowered to take incremental actions on their own throughout the creative process. Fledgling ideas are road tested early on, exposing dead ends and leading to prototypes that point the way forward. IDEO's concept of The Shop—the infrastructure that supports rapid iteration—can be replicated by any team through tools like giant whiteboards, rooms dedicated to experimentation, or team wikis. Some Web development teams go so far as to develop extra "sandbox" environments that allow developers to add and play with new features and tweaks outside of the standard development pipeline. As a leader of a creative team, you should create an environment that allows premature action. Whether you work alone or with a team, a commitment to early action—without too much conviction—will help ideas materialize.*

---

* Our team conducted a small investigation into this topic, known as "The Purple Santa Experiment," the story of which is told in Appendix 2.

Kill Ideas Liberally

If you can learn to take action more quickly, you will reap the rewards of having more preliminary data about new possibilities. But the ability to act on fledgling ideas will help only if you also have the willpower to abandon them when necessary. When asked about their greatest failures, many of the teams I met shared instances in which a new idea came up and pushed a project offtrack—an idea that should have been killed once it was clear to everyone involved that it was a dead end.

The ability to expose an idea's faults and doubts based on data from early actions is a critical skill for productive creative teams. Often this force of skepticism comes from a few members of the team who tend to see the downside of ideas rather than their potential. Some might refer to these skeptics as "Debbie Downers" or "killjoys"—drains on the excitement in the room—but their viewpoint is incredibly valuable. Those of us who work alone must find ways to cultivate this skepticism on our own. Whether it means playing the role of the skeptic for our own ideas or engaging others to play it, we must incorporate this proactive element of doubt.

Walt Disney is known for his boundless creativity, not his skepticism. But it turns out that Disney went to great lengths to ensure that his creative teams vetted ideas ruthlessly and killed them when necessary. An article by personal development specialist Keith Trickey describes how, when developing feature-length films, Disney implemented a staged process using three different rooms to foster ideas and then rigorously assess them:

Room One. In this room, rampant idea generation was allowed without any restraints. The true essence of brainstorming—

unrestrained thinking and throwing around ideas without limits—
was supported without any doubts expressed.

Room Two. The crazy ideas from Room One were aggregated
and organized in Room Two, ultimately resulting in a storyboard
chronicling events and general sketches of characters.

Room Three. Known as the "sweat box," Room Three was where
the entire creative team would critically review the project without
restraint. Given the fact that the ideas from individuals had already
been combined in Room Two, the criticism in Room Three was never
directed at one person—just at elements of the project.

Every creative person and team needs a Room Three. As we build
teams and develop a creative process, our tendency is to privilege the
no-holds-barred creativity of Room One. But the idea bloodshed
that occurs in Room Three is just as important as the wild ideation
of Room One.

Through the use of physical space and clearly articulated objectives for the phases of idea generation, Disney created an extraordi-
narily productive creative enterprise that changed the world of
entertainment. In their book *The Illusion of Life: Disney Animation*,
Ollie Johnston and Frank Thomas, two of Walt Disney's chief anima-
tors, wrote that "there were actually three different Walts: the
dreamer, the realist, and the spoiler. You never knew which one was
coming into your meeting." It seems that Disney not only pushed his
team through all three rooms, he embodied the characteristics of the
three rooms himself.

The best practice here is to value the skeptic's role in idea generation. When you find yourself (or your team) rallying around a
brand-new idea or applying creative touches to a project, you must

summon a dose of skepticism to ground your judgment. You don't need to set aside three actual rooms, but you do need a period of scrutiny in your creative process. You also don't want to create too much structure around when you can and cannot generate new ideas. However, you must be willing to kill ideas liberally—for the sake of fully pursuing others.

In a rare interview in *BusinessWeek* on Apple's system for innovation, CEO Steve Jobs explained that, in fact, there is no system at Apple—and that spontaneity is a crucial element for innovation, so long as it is paired with the ability to say no without hesitation:

> Apple is a very disciplined company, and we have great processes. But that's not what it's about. Process makes you more efficient.
>
> But innovation comes from people meeting up in the hallways or calling each other at 10:30 at night with a new idea, or because they realized something that shoots holes in how we've been thinking about a problem. It's ad hoc meetings of six people called by someone who thinks he has figured out the coolest new thing ever and who wants to know what other people think of his idea.
>
> And it comes from saying no to a thousand things to make sure we don't get on the wrong track or try to do too much. We're always thinking about new markets we could enter, but it's only by saying no that you can concentrate on the things that are really important.

It is typical that in creative environments spontaneous idea generation gets in the way of following through on any particular idea. The wise creative leader understands that idea generation is a wild animal that requires a stolid trainer to tame excitement with a healthy dose of skepticism. You need to say "no" more than you say "yes," and you need to build a team and culture that helps kill ideas when necessary.

Measure Meetings with Action

Most meetings are fruitless. Amidst all the brainstorming, we must find ways to measure the outcome of meetings. While some of the greatest ideas and solutions come up in meetings, we often fail to connect these ideas to a tangible set of next steps. Ideally, meetings should lead to ideas that are captured as Action Steps and then assigned to individuals together with deadlines.

Meetings are extremely expensive in terms of our time and energy. When a meeting begins, the work flow of every team member stops. All progress comes to a grinding halt—and every person's effort to execute is put on pause as the team comes together. At the very least there is an agenda for the meeting, but all too often there isn't. And if there is an agenda, it is likely that attendees were polled for agenda topics and encouraged to add something—a practice that only makes meetings longer. The worst part is that most teams plan meetings as liberally as they drink coffee.

After years of observing teams struggle to balance productivity with the desire to meet, I can report that the most productive teams plan meetings sparingly. Using the Action Method lens on life, we can argue that meetings have little value without any actionable outcome. In most cases, leaving a meeting without anything actionable signifies that the meeting was just an information exchange and should have taken place over e-mail.

Here are a few practices worth considering when it comes to meetings:

Don't meet just because it's Monday. Abolish automatic meetings without an actionable agenda. Gathering people for no other reason than "because it's Monday" (or any other day) makes little sense. Lacking an agenda, these automatic meetings have the tendency to become "posting meetings," when everyone just shares updates to no particular end. If you can't entirely eliminate regularly scheduled meetings, at least allow yourself (or encourage your leaders) to cancel them liberally. In busy times when there is nothing actionable to meet about, fruitless meetings become even more costly.

End with a review of Actions captured. At the end of a meeting, take a few moments to go around and review the Action Steps each person has captured. This exercise takes less than thirty seconds per person and will often reveal either a few Action Steps that were missed or a few that were double captured (leading to duplicated work). It also breeds a sense of accountability. If you state your Action Steps in front of your colleagues, you are more likely to follow through with them.

Call out nonactionable meetings. When meetings end without any Action Steps, it is your responsibility to speak up and question the value of the meeting. Ultimately, doing so will earn you respect, boost productivity, and preserve your team's energy. Just don't plan a meeting to discuss worthless meetings (yes, this has happened before).

Conduct standing meetings. Courtney Holt, the former head of digital music and media at MTV and now head of MySpace Music, conducts what he calls "standing meetings." Lengthy, pointless meetings are less likely to happen when everyone is standing—and gradually getting weak in the knees.

Don't call meetings out of your own insecurity. For team leaders, the true purpose of a meeting is sometimes just to get reassurance. In some cases, leaders who are unable to keep track of what their people are doing will call a meeting to figure out what is going on. Or, in other cases, leaders are uncertain about their success or decisions and crave a little positive reinforcement from the head-nodding yes-men for pure self-gratification. Having our team members in the room to report what they are working on is soothing. But addressing our own insecurities as leaders should not be so costly. As leaders, we should recognize the cost of calling meetings and identify other ways to build trust and accountability in our teams. Great leaders candidly ask themselves why they are calling a meeting, and they are fiercely protective of their team's time.

Don't stick to round numbers. Most impromptu meetings that are called to quickly catch up on a project or discuss a problem can take place in ten minutes or less. However, when they are scheduled in calendar programs, they tend to be set in thirty- or sixty-minute increments. Why? Just because it's the default setting! Ideally, meetings should have a start time and then end as quickly as possible. Some teams have experimented with calling meetings for ten or fifteen minutes and were surprised to see them end on time, even if they used to take thirty minutes or an hour.

Always measure with Action Steps . . . or something else. Sometimes, we must meet for a concrete but nonactionable objective. Whether it is to align goals, to sell everyone on a new change, or to address a cultural concern, meetings with a nonactionable objective can be valuable. However, meetings that lack both an objective *and* an actionable outcome should never happen. If you're not measuring the outcome of a meeting with Action Steps, then you need to measure it with something else. For project management meetings, value should be measured with Action Steps. For cultural change meetings, value should be measured with a shared understanding. And for alignment and buy-in, value should be measured with a new level of understanding and consensus after the meeting that will help improve the team's chemistry.

The Biology and Psychology of Completion

In April 2008, the Behance team held its first "99% Conference," inspired by the Thomas Edison quote mentioned earlier. In a world full of conferences dedicated to inspiring ideas, we created one focusing solely on their execution. As such, speakers were requested to refrain from talking about the source of their ideas, revealing instead their process and struggle in implementing them. It was a grand experiment: would people want to spend two days talking about the laborious and despised process of turning ideas into action?

The 99% Conference sold out, and a truly diverse audience from multiple industries attended. One of our featured speakers was the exceptionally productive author and marketing guru Seth Godin, known for his prolific blogging and numerous books on marketing and leadership.

Godin consistently executes. Aside from his best-selling books, he has created products, started companies, and founded a rather unorthodox six-month MBA training course.* Godin's abundant suc-

---

* Godin's MBA program is more competitive to get into than Harvard's. It is a small class of about ten students that experience a rather autonomous six-month education under Godin's direction. The 99% Conference was just one of many parts of the "curriculum." I have met a number of Godin's students and am impressed with their intellectual intensity and practicality. They are all emerging leaders; and I found myself envious of the experience they were having. As a recipient of a more traditional MBA from Harvard, I can say that Godin's MBA program likely serves as a better foundation and stronger impetus for entrepreneurial success than any other top MBA program.

cess has garnered a significant fan base that considers him a genius. However, Godin has a different take on his success. He agreed to speak at the 99% Conference to shed some light on his real track record and how, as a creative professional, he became regarded as successful.

His presentation had one slide—a collage of images representing all of the products, books, and other things he had created over the course of his life. He motioned to the slide and explained to the audience that the vast majority of the products or organizations he had built failed. "But," he explained, "the reason that I've managed a modicum of success is because I just keep shipping."

"Shipping" is when you release something—when you put a new product on sale, when you debut your latest piece of artwork in a gallery, or when you send your manuscript to the publisher. Shipping is the final act of execution that so rarely happens.

Godin made the case that shipping is an active mind-set rather than a passive circumstance. "When you run out of money or you run out of time, you ship. . . . If your mind-set is 'I ship,' that's not just a convenient shortcut, it's in fact an obligation. And you build your work around that obligation. Instead of becoming someone who's a wandering generality—and someone who has lots of great ideas and 'if only, if only, if only,' you are someone who always ends up shipping."

The reason Godin has failed so many times is because he has shipped so many times. At the same time, due to this mind-set, Godin has also shipped some marvelous work—trendsetting books and new businesses that have captured the imagination of the masses. But to ship with such frequency, Godin has had to overcome some of the major psychological barriers of the creative mind.

Godin believes that the source of obstacles to shipping is the "lizard brain." Anatomically, the lizard brain exists in all of us—it is known as the amygdala, a small nugget of our larger brain that sits at the top of our brainstem. "All chickens and lizards have is a lizard brain," Godin explained. "It is hungry, it is scared, it is selfish, and it is horny. That's its job, and that's all it does. . . . It turns out that we have one too." Of course, through evolution, the human brain has evolved into a complex system capable of thinking much more expansively—and creatively. But the primal tendencies of the lizard brain to keep us safe by avoiding danger and risk are still potent.

After the biology lesson, Godin explained that "every single time we get close to shipping, every single time the manuscript is ready to send to the publisher, the lizard brain speaks up. . . . The lizard brain says, 'They're gonna laugh at me,' 'I'm gonna get in trouble . . .' The lizard brain [screams] at the top of its lungs. And so, what happens is we don't do it. We sabotage it. We hold back. We have another meeting."

The lizard brain interferes with execution by amplifying our fears and conjuring up excuses to play it safe. Suddenly the responsibilities of our full-time jobs or our personal lives will support our lizard brain's call for retreat. While the lizard brain stays quiet when we have monotonous jobs with a paycheck for doing what we're told, it becomes riled when we start to challenge the status quo.

What creative people need, Godin believes, "is a quieter lizard brain."

Of course, it is extremely difficult to override our biological and psychological tendencies. To confidently quell the resistance triggered by our lizard brains, we must choose our projects wisely and then execute without remorse. By committing to always shipping regardless of success or failure, Godin is able to battle the barrage of excuses thrown at him by his primal self. He is comfortable with the risk of failure because he knows that such comfort is, in fact, the key to being able to execute. As a result, Godin has made ideas happen again and again. The price he happily pays for his successes is having a lot of failures along the way.

The Tao of the Follow-up

A big part of execution is persistence. When we rely on others to drive momentum, our projects are at their mercy. Sometimes, to keep moving our ideas forward, we need to relentlessly follow up with others.

Jesse Rothstein, an energetic and charismatic sales representative at Procter & Gamble, radiated the enthusiasm and collegial spirit bred during his days as a star athlete playing a starting position on Cornell University's lacrosse team. Working for Procter & Gamble, Rothstein spent much of his time on the road, traveling from store to store along the East Coast, meeting with the corporate buyers of Procter & Gamble's products.

Many of the managers and buyers at Wal-Mart, Costco, and BJ's Wholesale Club knew Rothstein—and they all loved him. But, while he knew everything about the trends and margins on toothpaste, mouthwash, and laundry detergent, Rothstein was best known for what he did when he *didn't* know something. He would seek the answer and ruthlessly follow up until he got it. Simple, right?

Following up is easy when the answer is a phone call away. But what about finding information that requires responses from multiple people? What about pursuing an answer that lies only at the very end of a long chain of frustrating and tiresome actions? Rothstein's gift is his ability to navigate corporate bureaucracies, multiple time zones, and various rungs of the corporate ladder to find information and serve his clients. He has no MBA, no souped-up technological solutions, and no magical powers. What Rothstein has is perseverance and a simple conviction that he adheres to with an almost religious fervor: he follows up like crazy.

"I'm starting to believe that life is just about following up," Rothstein confided to me on a hot August evening at a Thai restaurant in

New York City. "There's this one guy that I was paired up with to lead a recruiting project. It wasn't his real job, and it isn't mine, but it's something you do in a company to help out. It's corporate citizenship. The problem was that this guy didn't really care. I would send e-mails and a week would pass before a response. I would send drafts of a calendar for him to review and get no response. He obviously didn't care much, but the project had to get done. At one point, more than a week passed without any feedback or collaboration. So, I forwarded the original e-mail again. Then, two days later, I reforwarded the forwarded e-mail. Then three days later I printed the e-mail out and I sent it FedEx overnight, with my quick notation at the top: 'Just wanted to follow up.—Jesse.' He finally got back to me, and he did quite a bit of the work himself."

Rothstein's relentless commitment to following up distinguished him in the eyes of his clients and his employers. This simple conviction, he claimed, is at the core of his ability to pursue sales leads, relationships, and other ideas. Even outside of his work at Procter & Gamble, Rothstein put his follow-up principle to work. He started a nonprofit organization that runs an annual dinner fund-raiser called the 21 Dinner, in honor of a former lacrosse teammate who tragically died on the field. He was able to secure sponsors and well-known speakers from the world of sports, ultimately raising $50,000 in his first year running. It is no surprise that this dinner is now in its fourth year.

Rothstein later left a very successful career at Procter & Gamble to found a nonprofit organization called "Coach for America." His impressive ability to make bold ideas happen through great determination has enabled him to found such an organization despite a troubled economy.

To push multiple projects forward simultaneously—and succeed— you've got to have something special. People like Rothstein make you wonder if almost impossible feats become more possible through the application of simple convictions and practical methods like following up—rather than, say, genius.

After all, none of Rothstein's actions selling product at Procter & Gamble, securing venues for the 21 Dinner, or printing apparel were brilliant on their own. Rothstein's brilliance lies with the fact that he always identifies the necessary actions for each project and then takes them (and enforces them) relentlessly. He always follows up until every action is done.

Further investigation of Rothstein's system for organizing projects and ideas—and Action Steps—revealed a concrete method to his madness. Rothstein's approach, though highly personalized for his own work flow and on-the-road lifestyle, incorporated many of the key elements of the Action Method. From the way he captured ideas and subsequent actions in every meeting to the way he processed them, Rothstein rarely missed a beat.

There are many stories like Rothstein's among idea generators who follow through and are successful. At the core of each story, we find the same set of methods and convictions again and again. While each person's system is personalized, the mechanics of how productively creative people work are fairly consistent.

Seek Constraints

Sometimes I ask teams to tell me about projects that were especially difficult to execute. A surprising number of stories have a similar beginning: "The client was very hands-off." "There was no defined budget; we were told to think big." "The brief was rather open and there was no firm deadline established." While the outcomes may vary, the beginnings of these nightmare projects share a common theme: the teams felt especially free.

Sometimes this sense of freedom is really a symptom of something missing. Perhaps the client is still wavering about direction or awaiting more information from higher-ups. In such cases, while the brief may appear very open, the client is likely to impose more unexpected restrictions later on in the project. Such surprises are likely to cause frustration and redundant work. But this is not the main reason why open-ended projects fail.

It turns out that constraints—whether they are deadlines, budgets, or highly specific creative briefs—help us manage our energy and execute ideas. While our creative side intuitively seeks freedom and openness—blue-sky projects—our productivity desperately requires restrictions.

During the summer of 2008, I was invited to the set of *Engine Room*, a reality-TV series being produced by MTV and Hewlett-Packard. The program gathered four teams of four creative professionals each from Europe, Asia, South America, and the United States. These teams would compete as they addressed a series of seven creative briefs. Once the brief was shared, the teams would have anywhere from one to six days to brainstorm, plan, and execute their ideas.

On the set, I witnessed some miraculous collaborations take place despite extreme time limitations. Brainstorms were lean and ideas were quickly tested and, when necessary, discarded with little hesitation. Feedback was rapidly exchanged, and defined intervals of time were preserved for extreme focus during execution. The clock ticking discouraged team gatherings that weren't actionable. And the output was pretty remarkable given the time crunch.

Well-articulated problems can also serve as helpful restrictions for the creative process. At the inaugural 99% Conference, the legendary designer and Pentagram partner Michael Bierut spoke about his experience designing the sign for the new headquarters of the *New York Times* in Times Square. Establishments in Times Square must adhere to specific requirements to match the area's character. Specifically, the sign needed to be fifteen feet tall while not obscuring the view of the staffers inside the structure. Bierut tried to view the inherent design challenges as useful rather than frustrating. "The problem contains the solution," Bierut explained. His innovative solution embraced, rather than rejected, the constraints that defined the project—and the result was all the more gratifying.

The Pentagram Web site explains: "The answer was to break the sign up into smaller pieces, 959 of them to be exact. Each letter in the Times logo was rasterized—that is, divided into narrow horizontal strips, ranging in number from twenty-six (the I in 'Times') to 161 (the Y in 'York')." These pieces were then systematically mounted on the ceramic rods that wrap around the building to, when viewed from afar, form the letters. Critics' reviews were generally positive, and the project remains one of Bierut's proudest accomplishments.

Constraints serve as kindling for execution. When you're not given constraints, you must seek them. You can start with the resources that are scarce—often time, money, and energy (manpower). Also, by further defining the problem you are solving, you will come across certain limitations that are helpful constraints. As you find them, try to better understand them.

Brilliant creative minds become more focused and actionable when the realm of possibilities is defined and, to some extent, restricted. Of course, when you limit the realm of possibilities too much—by allowing too little time or budget—you will have to lower expectations for the outcome. The goal is to find the right balance, so that you can feed off the project's parameters rather than feel frustrated or unduly constrained.

Despite your natural tendency to thrive on untethered creativity, you must recognize and harness constraints. And it is ultimately your responsibility to seek constraints when they are not given to you.

Have a Tempered Tolerance for Change

In any collaboration, one of the greatest challenges that can arise is change. Of course, our ideas and projects must evolve with the feedback and realizations we gain over the course of development. While we must remain open to change, we must also ensure that changes are introduced at the right time and for the right reasons. Change can get us offtrack very easily.

When we become passionate about a particular project and invest tremendous amounts of time and energy, it's only natural that we become less willing to change course. Momentum and other sources of energy that help us survive the project plateau can also make us headstrong. As we become more confident, we also become more resistant to change—even when we need it.

Structure is a mechanism that you can use to preserve the possibility of change in passionate creative pursuits. Rather than invite consideration of change at any time, many creative teams set up periodic meetings throughout the development process called "challenge meetings." In a challenge meeting, anyone is invited to ask and answer questions like "What doesn't make sense with our current plan?" "What are we missing?" and "What should change?" This is similar to what happened in Room Three at Disney in the early days.

But change can also be bad, especially when it is the result of anxiety. Earlier, we learned about our "lizard brains" from Seth Godin and how, when we are nearing a project's conclusion and are about to ship it, we start to think of reasons to delay. Often, we start thinking of last-minute changes we wish to make. Godin calls this "thrashing"—the process by which everyone becomes a critic and starts to pick apart a plan, product, or service. Early in the development process, thrashing is helpful in finding flaws and further refining an idea. However, at the very end of a project—right before launch—thrashing becomes the predominant reason for delays and blown budgets. For this reason, Godin suggests that we thrash heavily at the beginning in order to avoid those last-minute changes at the end.

But what if, at the very end of a project, when everyone focuses on the final touches, a major flaw is discovered that requires significant change? Truth be told, ideas are most likely to reveal their flaws immediately prior to completion. It is for this reason that proponents of entrepreneurship argue that the primary reason small start-up companies have an advantage over large corporations is their flexibility and ability to make major changes at the last minute.

You want to limit change later on in a project, but you want to be able to change when you need to. You want to limit thrashing to the beginning of a project as much as possible, but sometimes a realization happens when you least expect it.

There is a delicate argument to be made about the benefits and costs of last-minute change. How do you differentiate between emotional doubts that surface and actual flaws? And how do you weigh the benefits of getting an early version of a product out on time (despite some flaws) against the costs of a later, more feature-rich release?

While you want to leverage the high level of focus and insight you will garner in the final stages, you also want to test the market and be sure to compartmentalize the self-doubts that naturally arise before a project is released to the world. Some teams will actually use the increased level of engagement prior to shipping to lay the groundwork for the next generation of the product. In such cases, the team is informed up front that all changes proposed at this stage—except those that take less than a certain amount of time to make, say one day—will be included in the next version. By doing this, you are able to make headway on a new-and-improved version *and* incorporate low-hanging-fruit changes—simple things that make a big difference—to the current project without compromising the launch.

Progress Begets Progress

As you successfully reach milestones in your projects, you should celebrate and surround yourself with these achievements. As a human being, you are motivated by progress. When you see concrete evidence of progress, you are more inclined to take further action.

To use progress as a motivational force, you must find a way to measure it. For an ongoing project that has already been made public, progress is embodied in the feedback and testimonials from the audience. For projects that are still under wraps, progress reveals itself as lists of completed Action Steps or old drafts that have been marked up and since updated.

Your instinct might be to throw these relics away. After all, the work is completed. But some exceptionally productive creatives savor these items as testaments to progress. They surround themselves with artifacts of completed work.

The inspiration to generate ideas comes easy, but the inspiration to take action is more rare. Especially amidst heavy, burdensome projects with hundreds of Action Steps and milestones, it is emotionally invigorating to surround yourself with progress. Why throw away the evidence of your achievements when you can create an inspiring monument to getting stuff done? Some teams, including the Behance team, have created "Done Walls" covered with old Action Steps. We literally gather up the records of completed tasks from projects—often notebook pages of checked-off actions and index cards with descriptions of features we've added—and then we decorate certain walls with these artifacts. For us, the "Done Wall" is a piece of art that reminds us of the progress we have made thus far.

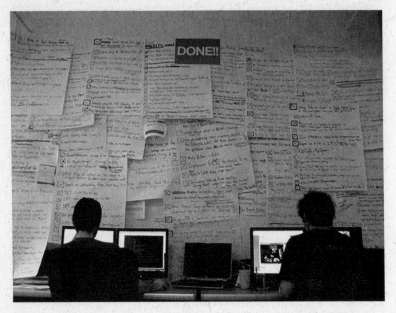

One of the past "Done Walls" in the Behance office, a motivational testament to progress

When we feel mired in the thick of it all, we can look up and see the wake of progress that trails behind us.

We all need to see incremental progress in order to feel confident in our creative journeys. Proof of this concept can be found in the analogy of waiting in line. If you find yourself in a long line of people waiting to get into a concert, you will notice that everyone keeps inching forward every few minutes as the line makes its slow advance. But if the person immediately in front of you fails to move with the rest of the line, you will get frustrated. Even if you know that the person ahead of you will move to catch up with the line later on, you still get frustrated as you see the gap of space ahead growing. Standing still and feeling no progress is difficult. You want to keep moving with the line in order to feel productive. The incremental movements with the line don't get you there any faster, but they feel great and keep you willing to wait. It is the same sensation as the one you get pushing the "Door Close" button in an elevator: even though doing so may, in fact, do nothing (many of these buttons are disabled), it is satisfying to feel you are making progress.

Feeling progress is an important part of execution. If your natural tendency is to generate ideas rather than take action on existing ideas, then surrounding yourself with progress can help you focus. When you make incremental progress, celebrate it and feature it. Surround yourself with it.

Visual Organization and Advertising Action to Yourself

It is no secret that design is a critical element of productivity. Design helps maintain a sense of order amidst creative chaos. It is a valuable tool for managing (and controlling) our own attention spans. Design can also help us advertise actions-to-be-taken to ourselves.

On a frigid day in February 2009, I visited John Maeda, the newly minted president of the Rhode Island School of Design (RISD), to find out how the leader of one of America's premier design schools organizes his efforts. Sworn in just months before in September 2008, Maeda was already making waves in the academic world, both for his nontraditional background and his bold management strategies.

For starters, Maeda implemented a plan for radical transparency—a topic we'll discuss later under the Forces of Community—between the RISD administration and its student body. The administration rolled out a series of blogs, including our.risd.edu, a forum for discussion about the RISD community that Maeda contributes to regularly and on which any staff member or student can post as well. Next, Maeda spearheaded the rollout of a network of "digital bulletin boards" strategically placed throughout the RISD campus. These fifty-two-inch Samsung LCDs present the community with information about events as well as artwork, photos, and messages posted by anyone on campus.

I was eager to meet with Maeda not only to learn more about his impact at RISD, but also to hear about how his unique background had influenced his capacity to make ideas happen. Maeda is a digital artist, graphic designer, computer scientist, and educator who holds bachelor's and master's degrees in computer science and electrical engineering, a PhD in design science, and an MBA. Prior to joining RISD, Maeda taught media arts and sciences at the Massachusetts Institute of Technology for twelve years and served as associate director of research at the MIT Media Lab. In many ways, Maeda embodies the new twenty-first-century hybrid creative thinker/leader.

Maeda's RISD office is a visual map of what's on his mind. The walls are covered with Post-its, sketches, plans, and programs of recent and upcoming events around the school. The space is quite different from any other university president's office you're likely to see, and Maeda admits it. "If you walk into my office," he explained, "you'll be shocked by it, but this is how I think. . . . I don't think it's the proper way for a president to decorate his office, but they aren't decorations. It's like spitting thoughts. . . . I want to see what's in my head." Maeda believes that to truly organize things in his life, he needs to properly understand them. And to properly understand something—anything—he feels the need to see it and work with it visually.

As we spoke, it became clear that Maeda believes the creative's ability to stay organized is not natural. Instead, it must be enforced using methods like visual stimulation and walls covered with thoughts, plans, and objectives.

Over the course of our discussion, Maeda jotted down many of my questions and comments on little rectangular Post-it notes that he carefully arranged on the table in front of him. Even as we

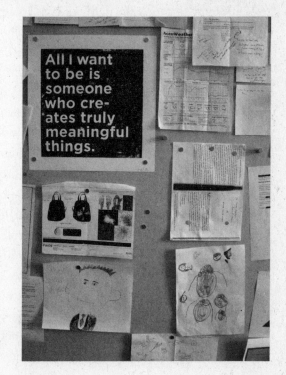

John Maeda's office
at the Rhode Island School
of Design, photographed by
Colin Williams

chatted, Maeda was organizing his thoughts and comments through a visual documentation of the conversation itself—a process that mimicked his visual organizational approach to all of the projects across his life. "You can only organize something if you understand how it works," Maeda explained.

The teams at IDEO, the legendary design consultancy mentioned earlier, have also made visual organization a key principle across their creative process. As you enter one of IDEO's buildings, you are struck by the free-flowing array of desks and computers—all personal workstations—in the center of the building. Employee bikes hang from the rafters, and glass-enclosed "project rooms" line the perimeter of the entire warehouse building. Each project room is a dedicated work space for a team of designers that has been assembled around a particular project.

While most visitors to the IDEO campus are struck by the creative nature of the space, I was intrigued by the physical dominance of actionable items and sketches on the walls in each project room. One team member, Jocelyn Wyatt, noticed my intrigue and explained, "We thrive off of being surrounded by what needs to get done."

Wyatt provided further insight into the nature of the project rooms. Staff members will write initials on Post-it notes for things that need to be done by certain people. Field observations and nuances that must be kept in mind during product development are hung up on the walls or on large poster boards scattered around the room. As I walked past these rooms, I imagined the utility of walking into a physical, three-dimensional to-do list and mood-board every day. When it comes to accountability and prioritization (and not letting anything slip through the cracks), nothing can beat this setup. Of course, when you're out of the office, you're out of the loop. Nevertheless, there is something to be learned from IDEO's very spatial approach to project management and taking action.

You live in a world of choices. At any moment in time, you must decide what to focus on and how to use your time. While prioritiza-tion helps you focus, your mind may still have the tendency to wander. When it comes to productivity, this tendency often works against you. Maeda, the teams at IDEO, and many others use visual design to or-ganize and understand information—and to stimulate action. As with the old adage "out of sight, out of mind," so we learn that right before our eyes, actions thrive.

When it comes to staying focused, you must be your own personal Madison Avenue advertising agency. The same techniques that draw your attention to billboards on the highway or commercials on televi-sion can help you become more (or less) engaged by a project. When you have a project that is tracked with a beautiful chart or an elegant sketchbook, you are more likely to focus on it. Use your work space to induce attention where you need it most. You ultimately want to make yourself feel compelled to take action on the tasks pending, just as a marketer makes you feel compelled to buy something.

MENTAL LOYALTY:
Maintaining Attention and Resolve

IT SHOULD BE clear by now that organizing life into a series of projects, managing those projects with a bias toward action, and always moving the ball forward are critical for execution.

But sticking to a schedule and maintaining loyalty to ideas is hard. Execution is rarely comfortable or convenient. You must accept the hardships ahead and anticipate the spotlights of seduction that are liable to stifle your progress.

You can only stay loyal to your creative pursuits through the awareness and control of your impulses. Along the journey to making ideas happen, you must reduce the amount of energy you spend on stuff related to your insecurities. You must also learn to withstand external pressures that can deter you from your path.

Rituals for Perspiration

Despite the many best practices of organizations with a bias toward action, execution ultimately boils down to sheer perspiration.

Roy Spence, chairman of GSD&M Idea City—the powerful ad agency behind brands such as Southwest Airlines, Wal-Mart, Krispy Kreme, and the famous "Don't Mess with Texas" campaign—was once asked by *Fast Company* magazine how he keeps up the pace amidst serious competitors vying for his firm's accounts. "The one thing that will out-trump everything is just to out-work the bastards," he proclaimed. "You've got to out-work them, out-think them, and out-passion them. But what a thrill."

Perspiration is the best form of differentiation, especially in the creative world. Work ethic alone can single-handedly give your ideas the boost that makes all the difference. Unfortunately, perspiration is not glamorous. Endless late nights, multiple redrafts, and countless meetings consume the majority of your time—all with the intention of breathing life into your projects. Passion for your work will also play an important role. Passion yields tolerance—tolerance for all of the frustration and hardship that come your way as you seek to make your ideas happen.

In order to channel your ability to focus—and perspire—for extended periods of time, you will likely need to develop a consistent work schedule. Structuring time spent executing ideas is a best practice of admired creative leaders across industries. It is the only way to keep up with the continuous stream of Action Steps and allocate sufficient time for deep thought.

It is worth taking a few moments to look at the work routines of some especially prolific writers of our time. Writing is a particularly labor-intensive exercise that calls for pure discipline and perspiration.

You can have all the ideas in the world in your head—or at your fingertips—but you still need to write them down, word by word.

In July 2007, Mason Currey, a New York–based writer and editor, embarked on a project to better understand how a writer's daily routine contributes to the ability to focus and execute. The project took shape through a blog, Daily Routines, that is scheduled to be published in book form by Knopf in 2011.

Currey chronicled the schedules that particularly productive writers—as well as statesmen, scientists, and artists—have prescribed for themselves in the past. For a year and a half, Currey's Web site had only a few dozen readers, who were mostly friends and coworkers. Then, in December 2008, the online publication Slate.com linked to the blog and Currey started receiving tens of thousands of hits per day.

Aside from Currey's own story of perspiration yielding a positive outcome, the interview excerpts and articles cataloged on Daily Routines offer insight into how developing a consistent daily regimen for execution can help us make ideas happen.

It was on Daily Routines that I discovered this interview with Michael Lewis, author of the best-selling books *Moneyball* and *Liar's Poker*, from Robert Boynton's *The New New Journalism: Conversations with America's Best Nonfiction Writers on Their Craft*.

HOW DO YOU BEGIN WRITING?

Fitfully. I'll write something, but it won't be the beginning or the middle or the end—I'm just getting an idea out on the page. Then, as the words accumulate, I start thinking about how they need to be organized.

IS THERE ANY TIME OF DAY YOU LIKE TO WRITE?

I've always written best very early in the morning and very late at night. I write very little in the middle of the day. If I do any work in the middle of the day, it is editing what I've written that morning.

WHAT WOULD YOUR IDEAL WRITING DAY LOOK LIKE?

Left to my own devices, with no family, I'd start writing at seven P.M. and stop at four A.M. That is the way I used to write. I liked to get ahead of everybody. I'd think to myself, "I'm starting tomorrow's workday, tonight!" Late nights are wonderfully tranquil. No phone calls, no interruptions. I like the feeling of knowing that nobody is trying to reach me.

IS THERE ANYWHERE YOU NEED TO BE IN ORDER TO WRITE?

No, I've written in every conceivable circumstance. I like writing in my office, which is an old redwood cabin about a hundred yards from my house in Berkeley. It has a kitchen, a little bedroom, a bathroom, and a living room, which I use as a study. But I've written in awful enough situations that I know that the quality of the prose doesn't depend on the circumstance in which it is composed. I don't believe the muse visits you. I believe that you visit the muse. If you wait for that "perfect moment" you're not going to be very productive.

Contrary to Michael Lewis, best-selling novelist John Grisham has a more prescribed routine—and it was even more so when he was practicing law and writing at the same time.

When he first started writing, Grisham explained in an interview with the *San Francisco Chronicle*, he had "these little rituals that were silly and brutal but very important": "The alarm clock would go off at five, and I'd jump in the shower. My office was five minutes away. And I had to be at my desk, at my office, with the first cup of coffee, a legal pad, and write the first word at 5:30, five days a week."

Grisham's goal: to write a page every day. Sometimes that would take ten minutes, sometimes an hour; often he would write for two hours before he had to turn to his job as a lawyer, which he never especially enjoyed. Working in the Mississippi legislature, Grisham experienced "enormous amounts of wasted time" that would give him the opportunity to write.

As you glimpse these well-known writers' routines, you get a sense of the important role structure plays in creative pursuits. While each person's schedule is different, the purpose of keeping a schedule is the same for everyone. Living by your own creative tendencies, rationalizations, and emotional whims will not suffice. Sheer perspiration will come only from organizing your energy and holding yourself accountable with some sort of routine.

Reconsider Your Work Space

How you arrange your work space is a very personal choice, especially as you embark on creative projects. Your surroundings affect your ability to focus, and perhaps your propensity to think creatively. But the characteristics of a space that make us more productive—or more creative—can seem elusive. Some teams insist on open loft-type spaces that are shared by all team members. Other companies adopt a more traditional setup of personal cubicles or offices that provide more privacy for employees. While there are no set-in-stone best practices for the ideal work space, there are some helpful principles worth considering.

Different types of spaces support different types of activity. For example, in one recent study by Joan Meyers-Levy, a professor of marketing at the University of Minnesota, it was found that ceiling height affected how people processed information. In the study,

Meyers-Levy assigned one hundred participants to one of two rooms—the first had an eight-foot ceiling, and the other had a ten-foot ceiling. All of the people were then asked to perform the same task, which involved grouping items into categories of their choice. Those in the room with higher ceilings came up with a more abstract set of categories, while those in the smaller room proposed more concrete categories. "You're focusing on the specific details in the lower-ceiling condition," Meyers-Levy explained in *Scientific American Mind*.

Smaller, more confined spaces may help us focus more intently while wide-open spaces with higher ceilings foster a more unencumbered way of thinking. According to Meyers-Levy, "It very much depends on what kind of task you're doing . . . if you're in the operating room, maybe a low ceiling is better. You want the surgeon getting the details right."

Meyers-Levy is careful to suggest that the actual dimensions of space are not necessarily the main determinant. "We think you can get these effects just by manipulating the perception of space," she explained. Nevertheless, her findings suggest that, when we are conducting research or trying to focus on our Action Steps, we should sequester ourselves to smaller, more confined environments. But, when brainstorming or beginning a creative project, we should try to work in a more open space.

Other factors—like the brightness, noise level, and décor—are also likely to impact your tendencies, but on a more personal level. If you pay attention to how your productivity changes in variable work conditions, you can start to move around and change your work space depending on the projects or tasks at hand.

Be sure to preserve the sanctity of your work spaces. In an attempt to limit the spur-of-the-moment meetings that are likely to happen in an open work environment, you might want to treat your colleagues as if their desk areas had an imaginary door. While it is tempting to have an open environment with constant back-and-forth, sometimes the state of creative flow needs to be respected and preserved. Our chief designer at Behance, Matias Corea, supports the notion of an open work environment, but when he needs to focus on something, he uses headphones to send a signal that he doesn't want to be interrupted.

Your work space is your zone for both creative thought and execution. As such, the ideal conditions (and restrictions) for your space will constantly change. Develop an awareness of your tendencies in varying conditions, and use this knowledge to better manage your energy as you make progress on projects.

Reduce Your Amount of "Insecurity Work"

As you introduce your ideas to the world, you are bound to become anxious about what the world thinks. You will want to frequently observe the progress you are making and confirm the status of everything you've created. This is a normal tendency, even though the root of it is often an unfounded insecurity—a fear that you've overlooked something or will ultimately fail. While we all have different insecurities, most of us share a common approach to dealing with them: we seek information to make our anxiety go away. For some, this amounts to countless hours spent reviewing traffic reports for Web sites, scrutinizing bank balances and every transaction in your business, reviewing Twitter search feeds for your business, getting daily e-mails with every piece of data you can imagine—the list goes on. Basking in the data makes us feel better.

I call these daily (and in some cases hourly) habits "Insecurity Work." It's the stuff you do that has no intended outcome, does not move the ball forward in any way, and is quick enough that you can do it multiple times a day without realizing how much time is being wasted. While all of these actions are important once in a while, there is no rational reason to perform them so often.

Insecurity Work is a trap that plagues many creative leaders. Your constant need for assurance becomes a shackle on your productivity. Work you can do that advances your projects is replaced by work that merely quells your anxiety. New technology and ubiquitous online access have made it even worse. Information that could make you feel more at ease is always at your fingertips, and therefore, you always have a desire to access it—again and again. Why? Because, deep down, we are always wondering what we are missing.

To cure ourselves of the addiction to Insecurity Work, we must employ a combination of awareness, self-discipline, and delegation tactics.

The first step is to recognize what you do in your everyday life that is, in fact, Insecurity Work. Whether it is checking the same search terms again and again or constantly watching your e-mail in-box as if it were a boiling pot of water, pay attention to where your focus wanders when you're distracted from the project at hand. By consciously labeling your Insecurity Work as such, you will become self-aware.

The second step is to establish some guidelines and rituals for yourself. Allow yourself a thirty-minute period at the end of every day (or, if you dare, every week) during which you can go through the list of things you're curious about. Perhaps make all of these things bookmarks in a browser that you don't normally use—and open it only when allowed! Weaning yourself off Insecurity Work is akin to reducing your reliance on an addictive substance. You may find yourself craving the data (and self-assurance) that you are missing. And so, you will want to wean yourself slowly.

The third step, if applicable to you, is to delegate the task of checking on this data to a less insecure colleague who can review it with moderation. The colleague should be told to review the data regularly and—when necessary—tell you when something is wrong.

The purpose of reducing your Insecurity Work is to free up your mind, energy, and time for generating and taking action on your ideas. Insecurity Work threatens to weigh you down and prevents you from escaping the never-ending ticker of what the world thinks. To envision what will be, you must remove yourself from the constant concern for what already is.

2 THE FORCES OF COMMUNITY

YOUR CAPACITY TO organize and execute is only the first of three ingredients in the pursuit of making ideas happen. The humbling truth is that ideas are not made to happen through solitary genius or ingenuity. As our exploration of the forces of community will illustrate, other people always play a role in pushing your ideas forward.

It is no surprise that ideas gain new dimensions when other people get involved. Concepts are more quickly refined, holes in logic more quickly exposed. As you engage others in your projects, you become accountable for being productive and following through. The forces of community help you capitalize on feedback, stay nimble, and share the burden of execution.

Your success will depend on how well you harness the efforts of others. As you will see in the chapters ahead, you must be proactive in identifying who your community includes, and how to engage diverse groups of people with different perspectives. With thoughtful stewardship, your community will become the ultimate platform for your ideas.

HARNESSING THE FORCES AROUND YOU

YOUR COMMUNITY IS all around you—your team, mentors, clients or customers, collaborators, and of course your family and friends. Your community will seldom understand your idea in the beginning, but it will help make it real in the end. Every idea has constituents—members of your community who hold a stake. It is your job to engage and make use of your idea's constituents.

Those with a track record for gaining traction around their ideas are especially good at harnessing the forces of community. However, there is a common hesitation to embrace such forces. The creative process can feel tainted once you introduce the opinions and influence of others. Artists are famous for their spiteful relationships with critics, some going so far as to insist that they don't create their work for anyone in particular—as if the enjoyment of their work by others is simply a by-product of their brilliance. Similarly, entrepreneurs often struggle to incorporate feedback and build lasting partnerships in their endeavors.

The process of creation is deeply consuming and lined with narcissism. We fall in love with our ideas and become both certain and protective. We forget to spend time on articulating (and marketing) our ideas, we become less receptive to criticism, and our ideas stagnate in isolation. As we dig deep within ourselves, we lose the ability to tune into the needs and sensitivities of others—an awareness that is required for our ideas to thrive.

As we share our ideas with our communities, we receive feedback and support. We may also encourage competitors who may, at first, scare us, but who will ultimately serve to make us work harder.

While I have based my assertions about the power of communal forces on the knowledge gathered from hundreds of one-on-one interviews, a growing body of scientific research in social networks also supports the importance of community—particularly in relation to productivity and success.

An article in the February 2009 issue of the *Harvard Business Review* cited a recent MIT study showing that employees with the most extensive personal online networks were 7 percent more productive than their colleagues, and those with the most cohesive face-to-face networks were 30 percent more productive. Clearly, our respective communities—both online and offline—play a critical role in helping us refine our ideas, stay focused, and execute to completion. In this section, we will explore how to best leverage the positive forces that community can offer.

The Dreamers, the Doers, and the Incrementalists

We all have someone in our lives who is a perpetual dreamer—someone with real talent who never seems to get his or her act together. Frank (not his real name) is a master carpenter with a love for his craft that started very early on in Croatia, where he apprenticed in the art of carpentry. He came to New York City with no more than his raw skill and desire to use it, independently, to build great pieces of carpentry—closets, shelves, and the like—for his clients.

When you talk to Frank about what he envisions on any particular project, his eyes light up. In his broken English, he will conjure up some carefully selected words to describe the fine details. "This is to be very special—you will like the fine edge, the touch . . ." And he will go on and on about the wood, and his plans, and what he might do after that. Jobs never have a scope. For Frank, every job is simply a milestone in his rampant creative journey to design and build masterpieces of carpentry.

Frank's clients recognize his brilliance, but they all complain about the same things. His jobs are never completed on time. Something always comes up. Although he always has an endearing way of explaining the constant delays, it's clear that his lack of follow-through is the real problem. The projects he completes are all stunning, but they are few and far between.

Frank is a Dreamer—a member of one of the three broad categories of creatives we've consistently found in our research: the Dreamers, the Doers, and the polymaths who we call the Incrementalists. The world is full of aspiring entrepreneurs, struggling writers, and passionate artists like Frank who have the gift of endless creativity and who are eternally challenged by it.

Dreamers like Frank are always generating new ideas. As entrepreneurs, Dreamers often jump from one new business idea to another. Even within an existing business, they are always imagining something new. I've met a number of creative directors in the world of advertising who insist that it is someone else's job to keep them organized and focused, while they are simply supposed to generate ideas—to dream. The Dreamers in the not-for-profit world are idealists—and they are likely to become engaged in new projects at the expense of completing current ones. Similarly, Dreamer artists are always starting new projects, often considering massive undertakings with a long-term grandiose vision.

Dreamers are fun to be around, but they struggle to stay focused. In their idea frenzy, they are liable to forget to return phone calls, complete current projects, even pay the rent. While Dreamers are more likely than anyone to conceive of brilliant solutions, they are less likely to follow through. Some of the most successful Dreamers we have met attribute their success to a partnership with a Doer.

Doers don't imagine as much because they are obsessively focused on the logistics of execution. Doers get frustrated when, while brainstorming, there is no consideration for implementation. Doers often love new ideas, but their tendency is to immerse themselves in the next steps needed to truly actualize an idea. While Dreamers will quickly fall in love with an idea, Doers will start with doubt and chip away at the idea until they love it (or, often, discount it). As Doers break an idea down, they become action-oriented organizers and valuable stewards. An idea can only become a reality once it is broken down into organized, actionable elements. If a brilliant and sexy idea seems intangible or unrealistic, Doers will become skeptical and appropriately deterred.

Then there are the Incrementalists—those with the ability to play the role of both Dreamer and Doer. Incrementalists shift between distinct phases of dreaming and doing. When imagination runs amok in the Dreamer phase, the Incrementalist begins to feel impatient. The developing sense of impatience brings on the Doer phase, and the idea at hand is pushed into execution. And when the time comes to pull back and dream again, the return is a welcome relief from being buried in the managerial mind-set. Thus, an Incrementalist is able to bask in idea generation, distill the Action Steps needed, and then push ideas into action with tenacity.

You might be thinking that becoming an Incrementalist is the Holy Grail for making ideas happen. The transformative capacity of the Incrementalist appears attractive until you consider the inherent limitations. With the ability to rapidly develop and then execute ideas, the Incrementalist finds him- or herself leading multiple projects (and, in many cases, multiple businesses) simultaneously.

One great Incrementalist we met along the way is Jeff Staple, founder of the firm Staple Design, owner of the New York retail store and gallery Reed Space, fashion designer of his own clothing line, and brand strategist for clients like Nike and Burton. Staple's extraordinary breadth of ventures has earned him tremendous respect. He is an exceptional creative thinker with the rare ability to slip in and out of organization and execution mode throughout the day. But as we spoke about his accomplishments, Staple became contemplative, questioning whether his was the best route to realizing his full potential.

"I love the fact that we do so many different things," he explained, "and it keeps me excited and I wouldn't change it, actually. But I do question sometimes whether, if I had just done the gallery or just the clothing line or the design studio or the store for the past twelve years, where would that piece be today? Maybe we'd have thirty stores now and maybe I'd be retiring in South Beach."

Incrementalists have the tendency to conceive and execute too many ideas simply because they can. This rare capability can lead to an overwhelming set of responsibilities to maintain multiple projects at the expense of ever making one particular project an extraordinary success. In my research, I came across many Incrementalists who were known within their communities for their many projects but never on a global scale. The Incrementalist's brands, products, and ideas are seldom sufficiently pushed to their full potential.

While a Doer and a Dreamer are best paired with each other, Incrementalists can thrive when they are paired with either one. Incrementalists are the "O" blood type of the world of collaboration— the universal donor. After talking to many Incrementalists about their most successful projects, I found that they just need to be pushed one way or the other. A Doer will push the Incrementalist into more of a Dreamer mode when necessary, while a Dreamer brings out the Incrementalist's impatience and organizational Doer-like tendencies.

As we examine the history of spectacular creations and the leaders behind these accomplishments, some obvious examples of Doers, Dreamers, and Incrementalists stand out. Bill Bowerman, the former track coach who developed Nike's running shoes, partnered with Phil Knight to transform his vision into a business. In the leadership of Apple, one might call Jonathan Ive (chief designer), Tim Cook (chief operating officer), and Steve Jobs (chief executive officer) Dreamer, Doer, and Incrementalist, respectively. In the world of fashion, the Dreamer Calvin Klein had Barry Schwartz, Ralph Lauren had Roger Farah, and Marc Jacobs had Robert Duffy—three fashion visionaries paired with a world-class Doer as a partner.

And so, there is no ideal category. The Doers, Dreamers, and Incrementalists all have their own strengths and limitations. However, once you consider which type you might be, you can leverage the forces around you—potential partnerships, organizational tools, and other resources—that can make all the difference.

Understanding the tendencies of Doers, Dreamers, and Incrementalists is the first step to establishing lasting partnerships and collaborations.

Seldom Is Anything Accomplished Alone

We all have strengths and weaknesses as creators, and we tend to assume that we are bound to work within those parameters ("I'm just not an organized person," "I'm not good at managing clients," etc.). From our discussion of the tendencies of Doers, Dreamers, and Incrementalists, we see how everyone can benefit from a partner who acts as a foil and a complement.

If you work in isolation as a Dreamer, your ideas will swiftly come and go without accountability and stimulation from others. As a Doer, you may struggle to come up with new ideas and solutions in favor of becoming mired in the details. As an Incrementalist, you will likely conceive of and execute a raft of projects that eventually sputter and grow stagnant, short of their true reach. No matter which type you fall into, developing meaningful partnerships will make you more effective.

Of course, we've all heard horror stories of partnerships gone sour. These typically result from mismatched personality types or too much similarity of skill sets. For instance, a collaboration between two Dreamers might result in a project that's long on idea generation and short on actual execution, while a partnership among Doers can quickly become straight-ahead execution and organization without the vision and spontaneity required for breakthroughs. Partnerships must be formed carefully. But, when they work, ideas can flourish on a much larger scale.

There are many famous long-term partnerships between Doers and Dreamers that have yielded extraordinary results. One such partnership is between Jeffrey Kalmikoff and Jake Nickell, the co-founders of the online T-shirt design community known as Threadless. Starting in the year 2000, Kalmikoff and Nickell grew Threadless from a small side project into a $35 million business.

The partnership worked because Kalmikoff is a Dreamer and Nickell is a Doer. During the preparatory phase for Behance's first annual 99% Conference in 2009, I had the occasion to listen in as the two explained their relationship. "I'm always on to something new," Kalmikoff said. "I'll think of ideas for new businesses within our business every day. Jake keeps us on track and reins me in. Without Jake, we'd have nothing."

Throughout the conversation that ensued, Kalmikoff talked off the cuff, jumping from anecdote to idea to anecdote without always following a clear narrative. When his points weren't clear, Nickell would step in to refine or summarize them, keeping the narrative on track. Their contrasting conversation styles were a microcosm of their working relationship. Kalmikoff, a self-proclaimed "firehose of ideas," kept the company infused with momentum and spontaneity through a rapid flow of potential innovations, while Nickell sifted through the proposed projects, helped focus the team on which ones made the most sense, and laid the groundwork for execution. As the Threadless partnership illustrates, Doers and Dreamers fit well together. They are seldom threatened by each other because of their very different strengths.

While some people like to find a single partner and stick with them for the long haul, many other successful entrepreneurs and creatives—particularly entrepreneurs who are constantly shifting amidst disparate fields (from magazine publishing to e-commerce, for example)—seek out partners on a project basis, weighing complementary expertise as much as personality type and working style. One such man is Roger Bennett.

Bennett is both an idealist and a grounded serial social entrepreneur with a remarkable track record. He hails from the same English town as the comedian Sacha Baron Cohen, a.k.a. "Borat," and has a similarly gutsy, no-holds-barred approach to his line of work: the Jewish not-for-profit world. He has committed himself to investigating questions around culture and identity. Bennett loves ideas that, though they might strike everyone as crazy at first, seem obvious when they actually happen.

Bennett has founded a variety of culturally potent works with the sole purpose of strengthening a sense of Jewish identity in young people. If you are a brilliant creative professional and happen to be Jewish, you have likely come in contact with Bennett or one of his projects: The Reboot Network of influential people in media and entertainment; the books *Bar Mitzvah Disco* and *Camp Camp*; *Guilt & Pleasure* magazine; and the Idelsohn Society for Musical Preservation, the record label of remixed Jewish music from previous eras that is behind the critically acclaimed Yiddish-Latin culture infusion *Mazel Tov, Mis Amigos.*

For every project, Bennett finds himself a partner. Partnerships are so important to him that he doesn't pursue an idea until he identifies the right partner. Bennett's project partners have all been great complements to his personality and Dreamer tendencies. On his various film projects, he has paired himself with grounded producers focused on the bottom line. When writing his books, he has found partners with both organizational skills and a strong familiarity with the publishing world. When starting organizations—something he has done multiple times—he has joined forces with action-oriented professionals comfortable managing large groups of people. Bennett knows his weaknesses and strengths and is always on the lookout for others with similar interests but different skill sets. He frequents several spots throughout New York City where he constantly meets with people who fit these criteria—usually over a drink after work. These casual conversations with like-minded individuals serve as Roger's breeding ground for partnerships.

Then there are the partners that you hire—people you engage to complement a specific weakness. Over the years, I have observed perpetual Dreamers who only "made it" once they hired a real Doer whose job was to serve as a partner in creative pursuits. In the world of independent creative professionals, we often call these partners "agents." Many of the most well-known actors, designers, and photographers have agents—and they credit their agents with the balance and career momentum they have achieved.

While researching partnerships, I had the opportunity in 2009 to speak with the well-known twenty-four-year-old graphic artist Chuck

Anderson, and then, separately, his business representative Erik Attkisson. If you haven't heard of Anderson, it is likely that you have seen his work—he has been working with clients like Nike, Adidas, Microsoft, Honda, Nokia, and Vans since he was a teenager. In 2008, after a recommendation from his good friend and colleague Joshua Davis, Anderson decided to retain Attkisson's services. Handling the bulk of new business development tasks, Attkisson fields client inquiries, manages scheduling, and thinks about Anderson's career in the long term as well as the day to day.

Although Anderson had previously been handling the business side of things competently enough, bringing Attkisson into the fold freed him up to focus intently on the creative side of his work. But the decision to work with someone else still required some soul-searching. "It had been only me," Anderson said, "exclusively me, doing my work for the last four-and-a-half years." Ultimately, it was the appeal of scalability that made ceding some control seem sensible to Anderson. "I thought, maybe it's time to give it a shot working with somebody else just to see how I can push things forward and take things to another level. I decided that I didn't want to be just Chuck Anderson the freelancer for the rest of my life."

Partners are just the first of many constituencies to consider as you develop your ideas. They don't have to be financial partners or equal partners. Partners are there to complement your capabilities and rein in your tendencies. Once you select your key partners, you will want to think more broadly about other individuals—and groups—to engage with your ideas.

Share Ideas Liberally

He who receives an idea from me, receives instruction himself without lessening mine; as he who lights his taper at mine, receives light without darkening me. That ideas should freely spread from one to another over the globe, for the moral and mutual instruction of man, and improvement of his condition, seems to have been peculiarly and benevolently designed by nature.

— Thomas Jefferson, Letter to Isaac McPherson, August 13, 1813

The notion of "sharing ideas liberally" defies the natural instinct to keep your ideas a secret. Yet, among the hundreds of successful creatives I've interviewed, a fearless approach to sharing ideas is one of the most common attributes. Why? Because having the idea is just one tiny step along the road to making that idea happen. During the journey, communal forces are instrumental in refining the very substance of the idea, holding us accountable for making it happen, building a network that will push us to go above and beyond, providing us with valuable material and emotional support, and spreading the word to attract resources and publicity. By sharing your idea, you take the first step in creating the community that will act as a catalyst to making it happen.

Take *Wired* magazine's editor in chief, Chris Anderson, as an example. Anderson wrote the best-selling book *The Long Tail*, which argues in favor of a business model that capitalizes on underserved niches (à la Amazon or Netflix), selling a large amount of rare (or low-demand) items in small quantities to a widely scattered cross-section of consumers. In many ways Anderson's theories relate to how new technologies allow us to harness the power of the masses—and it's a philosophy that he himself embraces.

"I don't believe you can do anything by yourself," Anderson explains. "Any project that's run by a single person is basically destined to fail. It's going to fail because it doesn't scale. If one of my projects can't attract a team, I pretty much figure that there's something wrong with it." To illustrate this point, Anderson uses the example of his idea to launch a blog that targeted nerdy, tech-obsessed fathers like him.

Once he shared the idea on his blog, the project quickly attracted an enthusiastic constituency, and thus Geek Dads, a member of the *Wired* blog family, was born. Had the project not attracted a viable team within six weeks, Anderson says he would have shelved the idea.

Anderson uses his blog to share and "beta test" the ideas that go into his books. "My philosophy is to give all of my ideas away for free," he explains, knowing that those ideas "will be improved by a community that collectively knows more than I do." A case in point is his latest book *Free: The Future of a Radical Price*, which, like *The Long Tail*, evolved out of a feature article originally published in *Wired*. Using his blog, Anderson refined the concepts presented in the book based on feedback provided to him via comments and e-mails. In a sense anticipating his critics, an entire chapter of *Free* is "constructed around complaints or concerns or push-back," wherein Anderson directly quotes issues raised by his readers and then responds to them. By sharing his ideas with the community, Anderson begins to build traction with an engaged audience in advance of the book release while at the same time using the collective intelligence of his readers to hone his arguments.

In the corporate world, sharing ideas liberally is required not only for keeping ideas alive but also for maximizing resources. Within a team—or between teams—new ideas are often realizations about how to run a business more efficiently and profitably.

During my years at Goldman Sachs, I had the opportunity to work with Steve Kerr, the firm's chief learning officer at the time. Kerr had pioneered the research and first implementation of the "boundaryless organization" during his previous role at General Electric, leading the company's famed Crotonville initiative. His notion was that removing the traditional boundaries between departments and between the organization and its customers would facilitate the exchange of ideas and best practices.

Kerr would often talk about how "hoarding information is an integrity violation," making the case that failing to share a best practice with your team or department was essentially akin to stealing from the company. If you had an idea or some realization about how your team could work more effectively, and you failed to share it with your colleagues, Kerr would argue that you had stolen from the team. For this reason, Kerr advocated for management practices that supported broader idea sharing, stressing the wisdom of moving employees around within a given company in order to spread ideas more efficiently between teams and departments.

Within a bureaucracy, sometimes you must move people around and literally share people to share ideas. The same case can be made for all creative endeavors: our odds of success increase when we readily share ideas and seek out discoveries that have already been made by others in our industry.

The examples set by Chris Anderson and Steve Kerr are refreshing, but they go directly against the grain of some of the most celebrated idea generators of the last era. Steve Jobs is notorious for extreme privacy around innovation at Apple—both with the public and even between teams within the company. Students across the creative disciplines have always been advised by their professors to share ideas carefully. Certainly, the thinking behind patents and idea protection in general holds some merit. Given our great passion for our ideas, and the potential value of the good ones, our desire to protect them is understandable.

Nonetheless, my research indicates that sharing ideas significantly increases the odds of ideas gaining momentum and ultimately happening. Creative professionals and entrepreneurs alike claim that they become more committed to their ideas after telling people about them. The fact is that great ideas are plentiful, and very few people have the discipline and resources to make them happen. When your ideas are known by many, they are more likely to be refined, and you are more likely to stay focused on them.

As we saw with Chris Anderson, advances in technology are making it easier than ever before to rapidly share ideas. Technology has made dissemination easy, leading to more progress and accountability. Across industries, new platforms have enabled each of us to assemble our own networks and quickly broadcast our latest work. The prospects of sticking with a particular project and enduring the lulls of a project's plateau become easier with encouragement from our fans or followers via social tools like Twitter and Facebook. The potential of these tools, of course, depends on our willingness to open ourselves up.

Ultimately, most ideas die in isolation because they are not shared and, as a consequence, are ultimately forgotten. You have a responsibility to become more permeable, even if it goes against your natural tendency. You should share ideas liberally—if not for the sake of your own success, then for the sake of society. From the greater perspective, you should hope that your great ideas happen for the benefit of all—even if you choose not to execute them.

Capitalize on Feedback

As you share your ideas with others, you will start to see whether people engage (or not) with your ideas once they're out there. The level of engagement alone can shed new light on the value and potential flaws of your ideas. And as people engage with your ideas, they will develop opinions about them. Ideally, the opinions will result in an exchange, and this exchange will result in useful feedback.

The value of feedback is inarguable. It is a powerful, sobering force that can help refine good ideas, kill bad ones, and postpone premature ideas that are not yet ripe. But if feedback is so readily available around us—and so crucial in making ideas happen—why is there so little focus on it? Very few creative teams that we've met—

in start-ups as well as in established companies—place significant emphasis on promoting feedback exchange. And a lot of creative minds can barely tolerate feedback.

Feedback in the creative world is clouded by a unique conundrum that ultimately comes down to incentives. While the value of feedback is high, the incentive to give feedback to others is low—and the actual desire to hear it is often nonexistent. After all, the work you do to pursue your ideas is a labor of love. The last thing anyone wants is to hear harsh truths about a loved one.

However, the more enamored we are with an idea, the more we need this reality check. Despite the uncomfortable friction that feedback may cause, we benefit when we are able to tolerate it. Those who are best able to seek and incorporate feedback see it as an asset and, in some ways, a form of nonfinancial compensation. At the end of a project, they will request feedback from others. Simple questions like "How did that go?" or "Is there anything I said that didn't make sense—or that you would have done differently?" can prompt an exchange yielding valuable insights. It can soften the terrain for feedback exchange in the future as well.

As a freelancer or a manager of a large team, you can develop methods for consistently gathering and exchanging feedback. One best practice for small high-performing teams was taught to me by Steffen Landauer, vice president of leadership development at Hewlett-Packard. Steffen encourages leaders to send an e-mail to each person on their team—as well as to key clients—requesting a few feedback points for each participant under the headings START, STOP, and CONTINUE.

Each recipient is asked to share a few things that each of their colleagues and clients should START, STOP, and CONTINUE doing. People then return their lists to the team's leader (except for the feedback about the leader, which is redirected to someone else on the team). The points under each heading are aggregated to identify the larger trends: what are most people suggesting that Scott START doing, STOP doing, and CONTINUE doing? Isolated points mentioned by only one person are discarded and the common themes are then shared in a personal meeting with each member of the team.

I have seen this methodology for rapid feedback exchange (and variations on it) work quite well in small teams across industries. Feedback exchange needs to be simple and action-oriented. The START/STOP/CONTINUE methodology in particular is action-oriented and quick enough to employ multiple times per year.

Mechanisms like the START/STOP/CONTINUE approach can be adapted for any project. They not only serve to gather intelligence in the course of making ideas happen but also send a message to your community of collaborators and clients. The message suggests that you are open to feedback, that you are constantly improving, and that you are actively learning.

Some people we came across went as far as suggesting that feedback exchange is a powerful form of self-marketing and can cause a metamorphosis in the project itself. Noah Brier, the head of planning and strategy at the Barbarian Group, a leading boutique advertising and digital agency in New York City, is a good example.

Among the advertising and digital media elite, Brier is known as a successful strategist behind powerful brands such as Red Bull, Panasonic, and CNN, among others. However, in the larger technology and marketing community, Brier is respected for his continued microinnovations. Whether it is a site called Brand Tags that aggregates brand attributes from millions of people, or a weekly morning gathering of creatives that has become the international phenomenon known as "Likemind," Brier has consistently conceived and executed bold ideas.

According to Brier, feedback played a key role in both honing and expanding these two projects: "For both of them I was quite involved and spent a lot of time e-mailing every single person who asked a question. I think that personal contact and feedback [are] quite important. Being involved on that level allows me to get to know the people who are coming to Likemind and using Brand Tags, and helps me come up with new ideas for ways to expand."

While Brier gathers feedback from projects in the online realm, Tom Hennes, founder of Thinc Design, soaks up feedback on the ground. Specializing in exhibition design, Thinc has a knack for executing high-profile projects—such as the exhibition for the National September 11 Memorial Museum at the World Trade Center site (due to open in 2011)—that must build consensus across numerous constituencies. The firm recently worked in collaboration with architect Renzo Piano to plan and design fifty thousand square feet of stunning exhibits for the California Academy of Science's Steinhart Aquarium. A creator of objects in the physical world, Hennes stresses the importance of gathering feedback by looking and listening to the reactions his work elicits.

Whenever he can, Hennes finds time to stop by the aquarium to see how people are moving through the exhibits. "I use this time to really absorb the product of my work," Hennes explains, "to understand what the effect of the thing I've designed is and how that measures up against what I had in my mind. I use the time when people are beginning to move through the exhibit, because the first behaviors I see tend to be the behaviors. The first fifteen people who walk through will pretty much tell me what I need to know. There will be outliers—every now and then, something will change—but for the most part, either they're using it or they're passing it by, or they're not getting it. I watch those people, see what they're reacting to, and internalize it, because that gives me concrete tools to fall back on when I'm thinking of broad concepts. Now I know what something does to reality. It's only one exhibit, but it's the beginning of building that base of knowledge in my head that if I do this, I could achieve that."

As all of these examples illustrate, feedback helps to refine existing ideas, spur new innovations, improve your relationship with your colleagues and clients, and build a well of knowledge about what works and doesn't work that will serve you well as a long-term resource. Regardless of where you are in your career—and what stage your ideas are in—you should not only accept feedback, you should seek it out. Managers, coworkers, and clients have a responsibility to share feedback, and you should encourage them to do so.

Transparency Boosts Communal Forces

Nothing boosts feedback exchange more than transparency. Nowadays, if you wish, it is possible for everyone you know to always see what you're working on. This may seem a very unattractive value proposition, akin to working naked! Nevertheless, your ability to make use of many of the benefits that your community can provide for you depends on how transparent you are with your ideas, objectives, and progress.

Tony Hsieh, CEO of the online retailing company Zappos, has spoken extensively about how the microblogging and social networking platform Twitter has helped his company build stronger relationships both externally (with customers) and internally (among employees). When Hsieh made the decision to embrace transparency both personally and professionally by using Twitter, the impact was powerful. Hsieh explained in a post on his company blog:

> Because radical transparency was part of the culture of
> [T]weeting, I decided to give it a try and be as transparent
> as possible, both for myself personally and for Zappos. It
> was also consistent with [one of Zappos's core values]:
> "Build Open and Honest Relationships With Communi-

cation." What I found was that people really appreciated the openness and honesty, and that led people to feel more of a personal connection with Zappos and me compared to other corporations and businesspeople that were on Twitter.

By embracing transparency and [T]weeting regularly, Twitter became my equivalent of being always on camera. Because I knew that I was going to be [T]weeting regularly about whatever I was doing or thinking, I was more conscious of and made more of an effort to live up to our [company's core values].

A lot of people use Twitter to complain or vent, but I generally try to avoid doing so because it's not in line with our core values. What I've noticed is that it's also caused me to complain a lot less in real life, and because of that, I've found that my own personal happiness level has gone up.

By using Twitter, Hsieh creates a powerful force of accountability for both himself and his company, and at the same time he builds the Zappos brand by communicating with his community (or, in this case, "followers") in a personal and honest way.

A more public evolution of ideas also helps distribute a sense of ownership as well as further refining and testing viability. As you turn ideas into projects, everyone around you will bear witness to your progress. When you share aspects of your project during development, you will get real-time feedback and questions that reveal unexplored possibilities. And when you get distracted or go off course, people confront you about your change of focus. Your community will come to expect continued updates and will serve as a source of both encouragement and constructive criticism. Social tools in the workplace like Twitter, Facebook, and other niche industry networks are making the creative process more transparent.

Imagine new ideas gaining traction (or becoming stagnant) as a result of how your community engages with them. Parris Whittingham, a photographer who makes his living largely by shooting weddings, saw the benefits of transparency directly. After posting some photographs of a Brooklyn wedding on Behance, another network member, India-based graphic designer Archan Nair, contacted him about a possible collaboration.

With Whittingham's permission, Nair took a particularly striking photo of a dapper young Brooklyn boy and overlaid it with whimsical, brightly colored illustrations. He applied a similar technique to other photographs, and then he and Whittingham posted the joint project to Behance. The collaboration was subsequently noticed by hip-hop celebrity Kanye West and blogger Josh Spear, bringing Whittingham and Nair recognition and spurring a series of new commissions.

Aside from the collaborations and useful feedback that can arise from transparency, you are also likely to become more productive as others see your activity and help you make connections you would otherwise miss. Andrew Zolli, the leader of Pop!Tech, a well-known conference and social innovation network, spoke to us about how transparency has made him more organized. "I give up privacy," he explained. "I've learned that no problem that I might find embarrassing is unusual. If you're willing to let people access your life, they'll find what they need. I've open-sourced my life. My calendar, e-mail, contacts are all shared with the organization. I'm highly transparent. You can see what I'm doing as a partner."

There is an entire spectrum of transparency. While some methods and tools may lie outside your comfort zone, even some additional transparency can help you harness the communal forces around you. Your ideas will be shared more broadly—and those who care most about your work and latest projects will subscribe to that information. You will receive more feedback because everyone who cares enough to have an opinion will be tuned into your progress. And the countless connections that arise circumstantially will make all the difference in your projects. Although the process can be uncomfortable, you are more likely to focus and make incremental progress when an expectant group of colleagues, friends, and fans is watching.

Communal Forces Are Best Channeled in Circles

If you don't normally work within a group, you may want to create your own. Writers' circles are groups of writers who meet on a weekly basis to benchmark each other's progress and keep each other motivated. But such "circles" aren't limited to the literary world.

For instance, Claude Monet is often recognized as the founder of Impressionist painting, but the Impressionist movement, which was quite radical during its day, arose from a group of friends and fellow artists. The original circle included Claude Monet, Pierre-Auguste Renoir, Frédéric Bazille, and Alfred Sisley; it later expanded to include Camille Pissarro, Edouard Manet, Edgar Degas, Émile Zola, and Paul Cézanne. At the beginning, the original four friends often lived and worked together, pooling resources, inspiring each other to take risks, and learning from each other's mistakes. Monet crystallized the importance of the Impressionist circle in an interview from the era:

> It wasn't until 1869 that I saw Manet again, but we became close friends at once, as soon as we met. He invited me to come and see him each evening in a café in the Batignolle district where he and his friends met when the day's work

in the studio was over. There I met . . . Cézanne, Degas
who had just returned from a trip to Italy, the art critic
Duranty, Emile Zola who was then making his debut in
literature, and several others as well. I myself brought
along Sisley, Bazille, and Renoir. Nothing could be more
interesting than the talks we had with their perpetual
clashes of opinion. Your mind was held in suspense all the
time, you spurred the others on to sincere, disinterested
inquiry and were spurred on yourself, you laid in a stock
of enthusiasm that kept you going for weeks on end until
you could give final form to the idea you had in mind. You
always went home afterwards better steeled for the fray,
with a new sense of purpose and a clearer head.*

Despite prevailing notions of the lone genius, this story of how
the Impressionists, a circle of friends, spurred each other on to
achieve major breakthroughs in the world of painting is more common than you might think. Circles like this play a critical role in
making ideas happen across creative industries. In some cases, the
use of circles has been institutionalized, while in others, formal circles are nonexistent. Regardless, circles are relevant and hugely beneficial for all leaders with ideas.

In the world of business, the Young Presidents' Organization
(YPO) is known for its "Forum" system. While the broader organization has many thousands of members, individuals are assigned to
groups of eight to ten peers who meet ten times per year "in an
atmosphere of confidentiality, trust, and openness to share in each
other's business, family, and personal experiences." According to
YPO, "A CEO's job is often characterized as being 'lonely at the top.'

---

* Michael P. Farrell, "The Life Course of a Collaborative Circle: The French Impressionists," in *Collaborative Circles: Friendship Dynamics & Creative Work* (Chicago: University
of Chicago Press, 2001), 27–67.

The Forum serves as an antidote to that isolation." For business leaders involved with YPO, Forums provide the kind of advice, motivation, and accountability that you would expect from a circle.

A small leadership development network at Cornell University has employed a similar construct. Originally spawned from a 118-year-old "senior society," a group of younger alumni started gathering in small groups to share career aspirations and personal challenges. What started years ago as a small experiment for alums to stay in touch has become a little-known global network of hundreds of emerging leaders who meet in small groups—and all together annually—for the sole purpose of sharing ideas, exchanging candid feedback, and fostering a sense of accountability.

While most young professionals struggle to depart the security of a traditional career, the membership of this particular network of Cornell University graduates has a strong track record of defying the status quo to launch start-up businesses, found nonprofits, and run for political office much earlier than most. "This network has helped provide me more guts and more guidance," remarks one member. Like the Forums in YPO, the small regional groups that meet often in this network are yet another example of the power of circles and how they motivate us to take risks and then follow through.

Regardless of your interest or industry, there are some key success factors for circles. I have come to call them the "Rules of Circles," and would make the case that circles should be conceived, managed, and sometimes abandoned with these rules in mind. As you develop a formal circle or push a current group of like-minded professionals to function more as a circle, consider implementing these guidelines:

Limit circles to fifteen members or less. When groups get much bigger than that, people feel accountable to a collective rather than to each other as individuals, which is less effective. The other reason for this size is purely logistical: it becomes too difficult to coordinate and host more than fifteen people. Also, when it comes to online forums and e-mail chains, groups larger than this become too impersonal and make it difficult for members to speak freely.

Establish a clear and consistent schedule for meeting. Circles can be ongoing or they can be one-offs that meet a set number of times and then end. There are reasons you might want to consider either option: a group of screenwriters might assemble a one-off circle to track the development of a single screenplay apiece, while a group of young entrepreneurs might create an ongoing circle to discuss business problems and solutions.

Meet frequently and stay accountable. For people's personalities to break through, one-off circles should meet for a minimum of five times. For ongoing circles, the most common practice is to meet either monthly or biweekly. Regardless of frequency, it is critical that all participants are held accountable for attendance and timeliness. Circles should have agreed-upon expectations for attendance, because the goal is increased familiarity among members over time. If a member has more than the allowed number of absences, he or she should be asked to leave, since consistency of attendance can make or break a circle's system of shared accountability.

Assign a leader. Every circle needs someone to oversee scheduling and to confront members with inconsistent attendance who need to be pushed. Some members of a circle will be more apt to participate than others. The best circle leaders can engage those who are tuning out or struggling to get involved. In addition, leaders should facilitate the start and end of conversation while always keeping an eye on time.

Extend your circle online. With the latest advancements in social technology, circles can and should use online tools. However, purely virtual circles are at a disadvantage. Without eye contact and set meetings that start and end on time, it is difficult to uphold the commitment and level of candidness that exists only in a physical and intimate experience. Nevertheless, every leader should consider taking aspects of their circle online—whether through online "drop boxes" that store files (helpful for writing circles that require the prereading of work), or online discussion boards that can enable offline conversations to continue online.

Regardless of your industry or level of experience, circles can support creative pursuits. Your contributions to your fellow circle participants will strengthen the collective value of the circle experience. Like most other relationships in life, the benefits you reap from circles are a function of what you contribute.

Another interesting dynamic that may arise within a circle—or elsewhere in your life—is competition. Among peers within the same industry, you will start to feel pressure to further pursue and refine your ideas as others share their own progress. These competitive vibes can act as positive motivators.

Seek Competition

Six years is 2,190 days. While spectacular creative achievements take time, Noah Kalina's "Everyday" project was unique in the consistency required and the forces that made it a worldwide sensation. Kalina is the first to admit that his idea to take one picture of himself every day—now for nine years running—was neither bold nor ambitious.

Every night, Kalina would snap two self-portraits with a digital camera before going to bed. On August 27, 2006, Kalina uploaded a video entitled "Everyday" to YouTube. The video featured the first six years' worth of self-portraits played in a continuous stream, accompanied by a soundtrack by his then-girlfriend and fellow Brooklyn native Carly Comando. "Everyday" became one of the top ten YouTube videos of all time, watched by over fourteen million people. Noah's fledgling idea—and the preceding commitment to pursue it—became art and inspiration for people around the world. An endless set of appearances followed the release of the video, including coverage by *Good Morning America*, *CBS Evening News*, *ABC News*, VH1, the *New York Times*, the *Washington Post*, and the *Los Angeles Times*, giving his career as a photographer a major boost.

Kalina's idea to document his life through daily snapshots became a major multiyear project made up of a single daily task. However, contrary to what millions of viewers might think, Kalina began with no specific plans for this project. Even years into taking the photographs, he didn't know how (or if) this particular project would ever be presented to others. It was just an idea—a creative project—that only took a few minutes every day to implement. While the forces of organization and self-discipline kept Kalina on task, the project was just a solo adventure until another force—competition—entered the mix. One evening, while exploring various blogs in the photography community, Kalina happened upon a video made by photographer Ahree Lee, who had made a montage of three years of her own daily self-portraits.

Kalina took photos of himself for six years before he had the impetus to aggregate them into what became one of the most popular viral videos of all time. Perhaps surprisingly, the impetus was not the momentum of the project or encouragement from friends or colleagues—it was Ahree Lee. Kalina saw Lee's video and knew he could present something even richer. Lee's project served as a powerful catalyst for action. What followed was a determined effort to present his project to the world. There were other photographers out there aggregating their own sets of daily photographs, but Kalina's pursuit encompassed many years, and he was going to make sure it got noticed.

Without Kalina's commitment to the daily tasks of taking self-portraits, the project would never have gone on as long as it did. Without the force of competition from Lee, the project never would have been transformed into something that would help his career. Without the collaboration with Comando on the soundtrack, the video might never have achieved the same impact. Kalina's idea was not necessarily novel, but the dedication and discipline that it represented was stunning. And without the catalyst of competition, who knows when he would have presented his project to the world?

Ideas often have the tendency to lie stagnant until we are jolted into action by either excitement or fear. The prospect of someone else completing and receiving fanfare for an idea that you had first is outright painful. Ideas are sacred realizations born out of our deepest sense of identity and wonderment. One might argue that our ideas are an extension of who we are and who we hope to become. This is why competition taps into something almost primal—the Darwinian struggle for survival.

For this reason, competition—regardless of whether it stems from friendly camaraderie or outright envy—is an extremely powerful motivating force. It serves as a catalyst for taking action and pushes us to improve our overall level of performance. Any leader can easily lose focus without a group of competitors to keep him or her on track. The competitive forces around you will display better ways of doing things. Watch them—and get to know them—rather than pretend they don't exist. While it may be against your nature to do so, you should actively seek out competition and be grateful for it. By embracing competition, you stay at the top of your game.

Commit Yourself in Order to Commit Others

When you launch a new project, you want everyone you know to help get the word out. You will want introductions to potential clients and customers. Ultimately, you will want your community to mine their Rolodexes and resources to help your idea gain traction. But a problem emerges if you have not yet demonstrated your full commitment to the idea you are broadcasting.

An example that comes to mind is Rebecca (not her real name), an aspiring jewelry designer in New York City who came to me for advice on launching her new venture. Rebecca had developed an extraordinary line of jewelry in her spare time on the weekends that was receiving great feedback from early customers. She also had just received a few great blog reviews on the line that, in turn, had led to more Web site traffic and some unexpected sales. She was becoming more confident in the potential of her business and was starting to take the pursuit more seriously.

As she posed thoughtful questions and jotted down my suggestions, I was impressed by her determination. As our conversation continued, I started to consider what I might be able to do to help—and who I might be able to introduce to Rebecca. At the time, Behance's reach in the world of jewelry design was really growing. Perhaps I could write an article about Rebecca's pursuit or introduce her to some great boutique owners who could really help launch the line? But as impressed and excited as I was for Rebecca, I had one reservation holding me back: Rebecca had not yet fully committed to the venture. Her full-time job as an analyst in an investment bank was still consuming the majority of her time. She had even shared with me that some of her recent orders were too large to fill. She was scrambling to improve her Web site and hire some part-time people to help assemble the jewelry in the limited spare time she had.

My greatest concern was that Rebecca wouldn't be able to handle the introductions or opportunities I wanted to provide. This would reflect poorly on her—and perhaps on me if I made the introduction. Was she really willing to take the leap from a steady career to one that involved more risk? Was Rebecca really going to pour her heart into it? As I probed further, it seemed I was not the only connection that was on deck for Rebecca. We were all waiting for her to commit before we did everything possible to help.

When you publicly commit yourself and take on risk to make an idea happen, you garner what I have come to call "Committal Benefits." Committal Benefits represent the increased likelihood of others to take a risk of their own—financially or with their reputations—to support your projects.

When I ask the leaders of new companies about the turning points in their success, they often talk about the moment when they informed their network of the drastic change (and thus risk) they had decided to make in their lives—the e-mail they sent to their friends and family announcing the decision or the blog post they wrote about the reasons for their transition. Only after publicly committing themselves did they experience full support from their communities.

When you commit, your community will be more willing to commit resources to help you. While it is okay—and perhaps even advisable—to tinker with your ideas for a while before taking the plunge, you must recognize that your community will not rally behind you until you fully commit yourself.

Create Systems for Accountability

Perhaps the most critical of all communal forces is accountability. Given all of the tendencies of the creative mind that we have discussed, it is no surprise that we need help staying focused and committed to our goals. There are multiple ways for us to create a system of accountability for ourselves. At the annual TED (Technology, Entertainment, Design) conference, the power of the stage helps hold leaders accountable to bold goals. Various online social networks provide tools for artists to broadcast their work. For freelance and remote workers, the coworking movement provides a communal work space that fosters focus.

The Pressure of the Spotlight

It is 8:30 A.M. on a crisp Tuesday morning in Long Beach, California. Approximately nine hundred people have traveled here from around the world for the annual TED conference. Leaders in the worlds of technology, entertainment, and design have come for a curated set of eighteen-minute presentations on new ideas and breakthroughs across industries. They have also made the trek to meet each other during the breaks and dinners that happen over the course of the five-day conference.

The audience is star-studded. From tech legends like Bill Gates, Steve Wozniak, and Google founders Larry Page and Sergey Brin, to entertainment icons like Robin Williams and Ben Affleck, everyone has come to indulge themselves with a healthy dose of wonderment. TED's tagline is "ideas worth spreading." As chief curator Chris Anderson (not to be confused with *Wired*'s Chris Anderson) explains, the purpose is "to put great people on the TED stage and let the rest happen as it will." But the larger collective hope is that some of the most important and timely ideas will gain the spotlight, and gain some momentum as well. Unlike most conferences, most people in the room at TED have the rare combination of bold ideas and the resources and influence to do something about them.

But the great potential of such brilliant people with ideas and resources would be squandered without any accountability. Luckily, there is a mechanism called the TED Prize, awarded every year to three people who have become leaders in their fields of interest. According to the official Web site, the TED Prize was "designed to leverage the TED community's exceptional array of talent and resources. It is awarded annually to three exceptional individuals who each receive $100,000 and, much more important, the granting of 'One Wish to Change the World.'" The TED Prize recipients are identified several months prior to the annual TED Conference and are asked to prepare an eighteen-minute presentation about their "wish" for the award ceremony during the conference.

Past TED Prize recipients have included former president Bill Clinton, scientist E. O. Wilson, U2 front-man Bono, and Jill Tarter, director of the SETI Institute, a global scientific organization in search of extraterrestrial intelligence. All recipients have a few things in common: they are leaders in their industries, they have bold wishes for the world (whether it is to fight AIDS in Africa or preserve Earth's biodiversity), and they have the resources and networks to actively pursue these wishes. In fact, the TED Prize recipients themselves might be the most equipped and well-positioned people in the world to pursue the wishes that they share with the TED audience.

As the TED Prize recipients come to the stage, one by one, to accept the prize and present their wish to the world, an audience of industry titans listens intently. Between each new presentation, a video rolls with an update on progress made in accomplishing the previous year's wishes. The combination of an influential audience and updates on the progress of past wishes creates a very powerful yet unspoken sense of accountability for the new recipients. Every TED Prize recipient knows that, one year later, they will be showing their progress to the TED audience and the broader world.

The TED Prize is an example of how you can use the spotlight to foster focus on a good cause. Those around you play a crucial role in holding you accountable to your ideas. Even if you possess the resources and wherewithal to turn your ideas into action, you'll still benefit from the impetus that can only be provided by others.

The Power of the Network

As I was exploring the Web late one night, I came across the work of Brock Davis. Davis had published a project called "Make Something Cool Every Day" a few months earlier, and it was miraculously starting to receive tens of thousands of visits every day. Davis had proclaimed at the start of 2009 that he would create something new and "cool" every single day, and upload it to the Behance Network. What followed was an endless stream of portfolio pieces, each with a caption and some clever artistic twist that made you eager to see the next one. Through sheer consistency, Davis built an audience on the Network that would visit his portfolio every day to review his latest post and pass along words of encouragement. Knowing he had an expectant audience in turn fueled Davis to continue to deliver regularly.

What I didn't know at the time was that Davis was just one of almost a thousand creative professionals who had joined together, through various online networks, in a group called MSCED—Make Something Cool Every Day. The collective was largely made up of freelancers in the creative community who had a shared determination to consistently develop their portfolios, get feedback, and function under the pressure of time. Of course, this entire collaboration depended implicitly on the accountability provided by other participants as well as by hundreds of thousands of visitors from around the world who were captivated by the consistency and originality of the work being uploaded daily.

The power of accountability comes from your community—those

around you who have a vested interest in your work and life. As you have learned from our discussion of the benefits of transparency and joining or creating circles of peers, your accountability to your own ideas is greatly amplified when you "go public" on any project—and even more so when you publicly proclaim your goals.

The Benefits of a Shared Work Space

In the traditional corporate world, the hierarchy within teams and the forces of face time, repeated check-in meetings, and bureaucratic project management tools are all sources of accountability. There is value in having someone look over your shoulder. Sometimes we need a push.

However, many of the mechanisms for accountability in the traditional corporate setting are overly burdensome, demotivating, and antiquated. A new set of technologies now enables us to stay accountable to our colleagues and managers without having to stay in plain sight. We can access our e-mail and schedule from anywhere in the world. In theory, we can always be reached. In some ways, the avenues of accountability provided by technology also enable us to live freer, more flexible lives.

To understand how systems for accountability can be incorporated into a flexible work flow that suits idea generation, we should examine the emerging movement known as "coworking."

The notion of coworking is very simple. Professionals across industries—whether freelance or full-time telecommuters—gather in a neutral space to work together. It can be a coffee shop or an open office space that rents out desks. While the professionals may never collaborate, they share a work environment that fosters focus and professionalism. In some ways, coworking provides the benefits of an office environment without the costs. There is no boss on site, no face time, and no office politics. But everyone feels a slight pressure to stay focused. In addition, the exchange of best practices and the impromptu collaborations that are supposed to happen in the classic work environment flourish even more so among disparate coworkers.

Tony Bacigalupo was an early proponent of the coworking movement in New York City and ultimately founded a physical coworking environment called "New Work City" that a number of freelancers and telecommuters from across industries use on a daily basis. Bacigalupo believes that coworking is the answer for any creative mind that is pursuing ideas professionally. "We're social animals that will go stir crazy in an isolated space full of distractions," he explains. "More important, we need interaction with others and a motivation to stay focused." Bacigalupo's eyes light up as he describes the benefits when individuals working across industries gather in a single social environment—and how coworking is redefining our notions of the contemporary workplace. He tells me that, after a day of coworking, people often feel as if they've completed multiple days' worth of work.

Bacigalupo recalls a story from early in his coworking days, when he received an e-mail with a funny YouTube link. His impulse to fall for the distraction was overcome when he glanced over at one of his coworking friends, squarely focused on his tasks. "I felt socially compelled to keep working," Bacigalupo tells me. "There is such value in other people watching what you are doing—not necessarily your boss, but someone that you really respect."

But it turns out that accountability isn't the only benefit of coworking. Bacigalupo also cites both job opportunities and increased creative output as products of the trend, noting, "Many freelancing friends of mine have gotten gigs out of coworking, some have gotten valuable feedback from skilled colleagues, and others have started entire companies based on brainstorms that started in coworking spaces. Diversity of skills is actually one of the strengths of coworking. By bringing like-minded folks from diverse professions together into one place, you create a very powerful contingent of brainpower."

Seeking Stimulation from Serendipity

Some of the most productive creative minds rely on a periodic dose of surprise to stay stimulated. Or, as RISD president John Maeda once phrased it on his Twitter feed, "Diversity of opinions and circumstances increases the likelihood of 'happy accidents.' Serendipity comes from differences." Stimulation is not only necessary when developing new ideas, it's also critical when refining solutions to a particular problem. Your brain benefits from new angles that come from outside your point of view.

Some creative leaders credit past mistakes for creative breakthroughs. At the TED conference in 2008, fashion designer Isaac Mizrahi explained that many of his design ideas come from "mistakes or tricks of the eye." Mistakes are illuminating because they are unexpected. But you don't need to screw up in order to find randomness. Consider a few of the strategies we have seen in the field—all methods for prompting and taking advantage of serendipity in the everyday work environment:

Work amidst other fields of expertise. Coworking and efforts to gather people with varied expertise together in the same work environment will prompt unexpected exchanges. Much research shows that the intersection of different disciplines is the catalyst for revolutionary insight. In his book *The Medici Effect*, Frans Johansson makes the case that an explosion of insight happens "at the intersection of different fields, cultures, and industries." Among the many examples in Johansson's book is a spontaneous discussion between a fisherman and an architect that resulted in a new design for fishing nets that transformed the yields for Italian fisherman. Diversity of expertise sparks new ways of looking at old problems. To capture the benefits of cross-pollination, we must avoid isolating ourselves in heterogeneous work environments.

Take advantage of mistakes. When you do make an error, allow yourself to briefly continue down the same path. If only for an alternative perspective (which is sometimes difficult to get), use every mistake as a lens to see things differently. One of the most famous examples of discovery by mistake is the invention of the microwave oven by Raytheon scientist Percy LeBaron Spencer during World War II. While working on the development of a radar system to assist the Allied armies in the detection of Nazi warplanes, Spencer stood in front of an operating magnetron. Later, the unassuming scientist realized that the candy bar that had been in his pocket had melted. Further experimentation to understand this accident created an entire industry.

Another example is the invention of the Post-it note—the result of a batch of poorly developed adhesive. The adhesive, concocted in 3M's labs, was so weak and unreliable that it sparked the idea for a temporary adhesive—one whose weakness was, in fact, its greatest feature.

The mistakes that led to the discoveries of both the commercial microwave and the Post-it note could have been simply ignored—a ruined shirt pocket and a discarded batch of adhesive. However, in both examples, the creative individuals involved decided to take advantage of their errors. As a result, we have two inventions that are now used around the world on a daily basis.

PUSHING IDEAS
OUT TO YOUR
COMMUNITY

IT IS NOW easier to understand why ideas seldom happen in isolation. Ideas die quickly without the forces around us that keep them top of mind. If we are transparent enough, our ideas gain traction from the feedback and accountability provided by those around us. Every idea has multiple potential constituents, and it is your job to inform and engage those who can play a crucial role in your pursuits.

The value of communal forces is tapped only if you are able to market your ideas well enough to engage others. While the first set of communal forces we discussed was of the "pull" variety—pulling people into your process to benefit the ideas themselves—we will now discuss the second set, which is all about the "push." How you market your ideas—and yourself—will determine the impact you make and the breadth of community you will reach. Your ability to push your ideas broadly will also depend on how well you tune in to the needs and concerns of others.

Overcome the Stigma of Self-Marketing

On January 12, 2007, the *Washington Post* conducted a rather odd experiment involving a $3.5 million Stradivarius violin, a Washington, D.C., Metro station, and Joshua Bell, arguably one of the most famous and critically acclaimed violinists in the world.

A few days earlier, Bell had performed at Boston's Symphony Hall, where even the cheap tickets go for a hundred bucks apiece. But on this winter day, at the height of the morning commute, Bell positioned himself in the busy L'Enfant Plaza Metro station, dressed in street clothes and a baseball cap, and played some of the finest classical pieces ever written, such as the Chaconne from Johann Sebastian Bach's Partita no. 2 in D Minor, and Franz Schubert's "Ave Maria."

As Bell delivered a virtuosic performance, more than a thousand busy commuters rushed past him on their way to work. Nearly every single one failed to appreciate his skill, and only a single person recognized him. After playing for forty-three minutes, Bell had collected only $32.17. In short, his precious gift went largely unnoticed.

In some ways, it is deeply depressing that someone as talented as Joshua Bell could not break through the cacophony of an everyday commute. At the same time, people would likely have been awestruck by the surprise performance had they been given the right context clues—like a sign announcing Bell's use of a $3.5 million violin, or a velvet rope surrounding the performance area.

Clearly, marketing matters. But all too often, marketing gets a bad rap, especially when the product being marketed is you. Honest attempts to market your skills can be perceived as self-aggrandizing, so, out of fear of being perceived as self-centered or too promotional, we hesitate to market ourselves overtly.

Nevertheless, we can all agree that your ability to access the resources and opportunities in your community is dependent upon others recognizing your qualifications, your initiative, and your interests. After all, if nobody knows what you are doing and what you need to succeed, then you'll fail to engage anyone. A certain degree of self-promotion is required if you don't want to live a professional life that resembles the Joshua Bell experiment. If people are not made to recognize your strengths, how will they know when, where, and how to leverage them?

I touched on the trend toward a more mobile, independent workforce earlier in this book, and while researching the topic, I spoke with Sara Horowitz, founder and executive director of the Freelancers Union, an organization that strives to create a platform for freelance workers. At the time, the Freelancers Union was experiencing explosive growth, with its membership nearly doubling from 55,000 independent workers to well over 105,000 in just a year's time. More and more people were deciding to go solo, often abandoning corporate jobs in favor of a more autonomous lifestyle practicing their craft.

Horowitz acknowledged that freelancers across industries share a common struggle in marketing themselves. When you work alone, you don't have a marketing department or a team of people to make sales calls. "Freelancers need to spend half of their time marketing themselves and the other half doing their work," Horowitz explained. Without marketing, freelancers aren't adequately showcasing their capabilities, which can result in a drought of new clients.

But the stigma around self-marketing and overt promotional efforts runs strong among independent workers. Creatives, in particular, are often guilty of leaping into new projects with a "build it and they will come" attitude that privileges notions of undeniable genius over the effectiveness of smart marketing.

Horowitz believes that the difference between deplorable and sensational self-marketing is in the intentions. "Marketing should not be seen as fake," she explains. "At its best, marketing is building relationships—and learning." When you go to lunch with people, when you ask for feedback and develop a relationship based on mutual exchange of information, it is optimized marketing. It is optimal because the intentions are multidimensional. You're valuing the process of getting to know someone, learning something new, and, in the process, familiarizing them with your capabilities. Self-marketing, it seems, is akin to cross-pollination. You have the opportunity to communicate your objectives by seeking to understand those of others.

All of us can learn from the unique challenges that freelancers face. Since freelancers don't have a boss to reward (and build upon) strengths with new opportunities, they must proactively seek new projects that showcase their strengths. And since freelancers typically lack the resources to do PR blitzes—and hesitate to overtly promote themselves given the nature of their community—they must focus on marketing by building relationships. Out of necessity, freelancers take the responsibility for communicating their strengths into their own hands.

When you work within an organization, it is easier to depend on others to give you opportunities. When I worked with Rob Kaplan, the former vice chairman of Goldman Sachs, he shared stories of middle managers, disappointed after their year-end review and bonus, complaining about not being promoted and recognized for their true potential. They would blame their managers, but Kaplan would urge them to look inward instead. "Your career is 100 percent your responsibility," he would say. Marketing one's strengths, Kaplan believed, was ultimately a responsibility that each person had to accept for him- or herself.

You can't rely on others—especially your managers and clients—to engage your strengths. In an ideal world, managers would constantly be thinking about how to best utilize their people—and clients would always unearth your greatest potential. Unfortunately, the reality is that bosses and clients are as worried about their own careers as you are about your own. You must take the task of marketing your strengths into your own hands.

Once you accept responsibility for marketing yourself, you can start to mine for opportunities. Often, the opportunity to showcase your greatest strengths arises as a side project or extracurricular activity outside the scope of your official duties. Little problems pop up all the time that are, in fact, opportunities to which you can add a unique value. Fight the desire to wait for instructions, and learn to showcase your skills and expertise without an invitation.

Effective Self-Marketing Builds Respect

Not surprisingly, the serial idea makers who I have met are, across the board, focused on marketing themselves and their brands. In essence, each has developed a program for the purpose of self-promotion, but not in the way you would think. As Sara Horowitz pointed out in our conversation, there's something about marketing that sounds, or at least seems, inherently "fake." This is perhaps why the most successful marketing is not conducted as a cooked-up, one-off campaign, but as an ongoing aspect of brand development that stems from an authentic place. Rather than coming off as distastefully self-promotional, the best marketing builds respect.

Take, for example, Noah Brier, the New York City marketing strategist who created Brand Tags, Likemind, and was included in *Fast Company*'s 2009 list of the 100 Most Creative People in Business. Brier has maintained a blog at NoahBrier.com since 2004. Here, Brier records his thoughts on a wide range of subjects that interest him—everything from neuroscience and life hacks to business, economics, and creativity. In short, he doesn't write just about marketing, nor does he see his blog as a marketing tool. Rather, it's a sandbox for sharing and commenting on current events, proposing ideas and projects, and so forth. Because he is a strategist, the product that Brier has to market is his thinking, and that's what his blog does. Over the years, it has become a magnet for those at the forefront of digital media because of Brier's insights and interests.

Brier's blog is only one of many ways that Brier engages his audience. Many people have met or learned about Brier through their participation in Likemind. Every few weeks, creative people in cities around the world gather for an early coffee before the workday begins. These Likemind gatherings are coordinated on a Web site that Brier developed after teaching himself the programming language PHP. (The concept for the get-togethers emerged from Brier's habit of grabbing an early breakfast with people he wanted to keep in touch with.) Brier's blog and his network of thousands of creative people gathering for coffee have garnered him much respect, and deservedly so. That respect, in turn, fuels a valuable brand called Noah Brier.

Brier says that people often ask him if he's made any money off his blog or Likemind over the years. He has not. Money is not the point. However, he attributes many of his achievements and connections throughout his life to these projects. Over coffee, Brier went through the chain: he met Piers Fawkes, the trend forecaster behind PSFK .com, through his blog; he and Piers got Likemind off the ground; Likemind led to his being hired by Naked Communications; he met his longtime girlfriend while working at Naked; he met Benjamin Palmer (cofounder and CEO of Barbarian Group) through Likemind, and now Brier is a lead strategist at Barbarian Group.

Clearly, Brier's career has been fueled by the many projects he works on that engage people, increase their awareness of his skill set, and build respect. Brier's non-revenue-producing self-marketing initiatives have been—and continue to be—the catalysts for his career.

As Brier reflected on the interconnectedness of it all, he shared what he sees as a big problem in the media world. "People don't understand that 'monetization' doesn't happen directly," he explained. "But if you get people to visit you, and they find that they like the experience, other opportunities will arise." Brier wholeheartedly believes that people can visit you—and come to respect you—only if you put yourself out there in an authentic way.

A good self-marketing strategy should start with intrinsic interests that can become personal projects—projects that demonstrate your strengths. As your strengths become utilized, people will start to respect you for something that is real—something that is earned.

For the designers, photographers, and other visual creative professionals of the world, portfolios serve as an engine for respect. The ability to gather and present your past accomplishments visually in a "show, don't tell" framework is much more effective than having a list of clients or distributing a resumé. But the portfolio becomes an even more powerful means for presenting oneself when the work within it is not confined to a static personal Web site or traditional portfolio site. More modern network utilities like Vimeo, YouTube, Flickr, and our own Behance Network now serve as a way to stream your creative work to other Web sites and other people who choose to follow your work.

The concept of amassing a group of "followers" on the Web—whether via Twitter, Facebook, or on some niche online community—is something I have come to call "respect-based self-marketing." People choose to follow you and your work because they respect you or something you have done. Once they choose to follow you, they have invited you to push information and updates to them. The same approach should be taken offline. We should all be showcasing our strengths to amass respect and followers.

As you develop and launch your respect-based self-marketing campaign, consider the following steps:

Identify your differentiating attributes. Self-marketing should start with identifying the strengths that differentiate you from others. Are you a designer who has a unique background in computer science or some other unrelated field? Did you spend time in other countries or develop certain skills while working with a well-known client? Are you particularly young—or old—relative to your peers? Make a list of your most differentiating attributes without judging how they might be perceived. Remember that unique features can be regarded as strengths or weaknesses depending on how they are communicated.

Develop a communications strategy. Once you have identified your differentiating attributes, you will want to identify the reasons they can serve as strengths. How does your background in computer science help you as a designer? How is the time that you spent in other countries helpful in your work? Why do you find your age—or any other attribute—to be an advantage in your field? Be introspective and advocate for the unique perspective that you bring to every project and problem.

Execute your communications strategy. Now that you have your list of differentiating attributes—and the storyline around how they serve as strengths—you must find ways to share with others. You might want to start a blog or Twitter account in which you share your musings and ideas. Your candid posts about projects you're working on, articles you read, or ideas you have—and how your unique strengths play into it all—will engage others. People will likely respect the efforts you take and the decisions you make when they understand the source of your strengths and ambitions. While at work, you might consider volunteering for internal or side projects that will best showcase your strengths and take full advantage of your differentiating attributes.

For Noah Brier, this involved a continuing series of breakfasts and a few quick side projects that shared his perspective and talent with the world. For others, it may involve setting up a dynamic portfolio site, doing pro bono work for a nonprofit, or writing freelance articles for local newspapers.

Once you have a strategy in place for reaching out to the many constituents of your brand and your ideas, you will want to fine-tune this outreach for particular groups of constituents. After all, everyone has his or her own self-interests and sensitivities.

Find Your Own Frequency, Then Tune in to Engage Others

As we have learned, ideas are unlikely to happen without the participation of others: partners, potential customers and clients, critics, the press, marketing partners—the list goes on. The one sure thing about these disparate constituencies is that they are all truly different. They all have different needs, preferences, and insecurities. Clients are focused on one thing while critics, the press, and your creative-minded peers are focused on others. A challenge arises as passionate creatives attempt to connect across the spectrum. Your ability to connect with each constituency will determine the traction you gain for your ideas.

Consider, for a moment, the old-fashioned FM car radio, with its little knob for tuning into stations across a spectrum from 88.0 to 107.9. Each station has its own frequency, and as you drive along, you scan different frequencies to find your taste in music.

Now think of your favorite radio station. Whatever station that is, it has an exact frequency that you can tune in to for your listening pleasure. If your station is 106.7, you have little to no reception for this station at either 106.3 or 106.9, and perhaps only a subpar, static-ridden reception at 106.6 and 106.8. Needless to say, you would find any inexact tuning unfavorable. Static gets in the way of really listening and connecting to the music and the message.

"Frequency theory" suggests that we all emit our own unique frequency in our everyday lives. A creative mind intoxicated on the merits of a particular idea emits a stronger but narrower set of signals. Similarly, we are receptive to a smaller spectrum when our minds are focused on particular ideas. Brilliant creative minds become a single spot on the spectrum—102.3 or 98.5—and unless you're right there with them, you're unlikely to connect. Our frequency determines the other people to whom we are most receptive and connected to. As we stretch to connect with people at other frequencies, we must adjust how we communicate, present our ideas, and engage others.

Think about the many people you know and work with. There are some people, perhaps your closest friends and associates, with whom you are very receptive and feel an inherent connection. You can even connect with these people nonverbally. And then there are others with whom you share a more subtle connection. You can connect, but there is some static—something that limits the degree of mutual understanding. Finally, there are those with whom you sense no connection—you just don't feel any click. Perhaps you attribute this lack of connection to different values or having nothing in common.

It is no surprise that we prefer to gravitate toward people with similar interests and a shared understanding and appreciation for our ideas. We're simply more in tune with some folks than others, and hanging out at our own frequency is comfortable. We get lots of agreement and take solace in shared values and motivations. However, by doing so exclusively, we miss out on the full force that our community has to offer. It is only by connecting across the spectrum that we will find a diverse audience and a sustainable market.

One of the best things you can do for your ideas is develop the capacity to tune in to the perspectives of others—and to help others tune in to yours. Interaction, whether it is with an individual or an audience, can be maximized by understanding who you are talking to. What excites them? What are they worried about? Just synthesizing this information will help you further engage those around you.

But what does it mean to tune in like this? Does this chameleon-like behavior involve compromising your principles? Certainly not. On the contrary, leaders that change frequencies seem to be more in touch with their true selves. They are driven by deeply held convictions rather than by some persona that requires tremendous energy to uphold.

Connecting with people across the spectrum requires us to stay connected to the needs and beliefs of those around us. This becomes more challenging when we get lost in our own creative pursuits. There is no question that the creative mind has narcissistic tendencies. While helpful in developing ideas that challenge the status quo, these tendencies also limit our ability to connect with others.

You must create an experience that your audience will relate to, but one that ultimately presents your ideas and your sincere intentions.

You can tune in to others without compromising your authenticity or values by focusing on the mutual benefits of connection. What does your audience need and what are you hoping to get? This knowledge helps you articulate your real motivations and interests in a way that your particular audience will be receptive to. Receptivity leads to engagement—and ultimately to respect and collaboration. The greatest creative leaders, who gain widespread support around their ideas, understand this frequency theory. They acknowledge that we all operate at various spots along a spectrum of receptivity—and that we all have something to give and to gain. Their efforts to engage us in their pursuits are both strategic and heartfelt.

Ground Your Ideas Outside Your Community

We have talked a lot about the benefits of collaboration and feedback exchange with others on your team—and within your community. But simply having the support of a community of like-minded people is not enough. In fact, a community sourced from just one stop along the frequency spectrum can prove damaging. Without some degree of mass appeal, most ideas will falter.

There is an unfortunate fact about the world of innovation: the vast majority of new products fail, most new companies and restaurants close their doors in the first two years, and most new ad campaigns don't achieve their objectives. In his book *Crossing the Chasm*, marketing expert Geoffrey Moore explores the giant gap between the early adopters of anything new, and the "pragmatists"—those in the majority that are more skeptical and risk-averse.

The root of the problem is the visionary's tendency to focus on what fellow open-minded early-adopting visionaries value. All too often, creative people make stuff for creative people. This is especially apparent in the advertising industry, where it is widely known that cutting-edge, award-winning campaigns often fail to meet client goals. After all, the judges for awards are not average consumers from Middle America but rather other creative professionals. People in one isolated spot on the frequency spectrum will be especially receptive in that area—and this is a liability when vetting ideas. Some companies in search of effective advertising campaigns avoid working with award-winning firms in favor of more grounded (and perhaps less imaginative) commercially focused firms that are less likely to lose touch with the masses.

When you conceive new ideas and execute them, you must assume a pragmatic lens that grounds your expectations, tastes, and perceptions. Don't confine yourself to one very comfortable spot along the frequency spectrum as you seek to share your ideas and get feedback. The most productive creative professionals and teams in the world have found strategies to cross the chasm.

One best practice is to ground every creative process with diversity. Engaging a few cynical, risk-averse advisers or members of a team will add a valuable chemistry to the creative process that may reduce "idea intoxication." You need to work with people who ask the difficult, practical questions that are frustrating but important when pushing ideas forward.

I have met others along the way who take an "ask your mom" approach. I don't want to suggest that your mom isn't with it, but polling an aloof or disconnected audience can be a bracing way to gauge your idea's potential traction. Does the average person see what you see? Can the average person understand the value proposition that you are offering with your new idea?

Yet another best practice is to preserve a week of skepticism between an idea and the decision to take action. With a pause between ideation and action, the energy in a creative process will either die or thrive. Of course, if you jump on an idea right away, you may capture energy that would otherwise disappear as an idea matures. But in such cases, creative teams often pursue half-baked ideas that may yield poor outcomes. Instead, create a sacred space for an idea to stand the test of time. After a week, you may realize that your idea has no legs. Such realizations will save you precious energy and help your other projects get the attention they deserve.

Recognize When You Are No Longer a Solo Show

As you seek to engage others in your endeavors, you'll need to overcome the default mode of self-reliance that is so common among creative people. Many entrepreneurs and other creatives fondly recall a childhood in which, amidst overbearing siblings or other family challenges, they would largely entertain themselves, working on creative projects in isolation. This self-reliance may have fostered their creativity, but it became a hindrance when it was time to scale, engage partners, and build a team.

Self-starters are often successful doing everything themselves. However, when forced to grow beyond the one-person show, many creative people struggle to make the leap from a solo success to a successful collaboration.

The transition from running with your own ideas to working with a creative team can be painful. The skills needed to lead your self (primarily self-reliance) are quite different from the skills required to lead others. Once the best candidate for every task, you can become a victim of your own talents as you are forced to delegate, share ownership, and "let things go."

The first symptom of an inability to scale is finding yourself doing things that can be done by others (although, admittedly not quite as well). Yes, it is always ideal when the head designer, the company founder, or the architect with her or his name on the door can deal directly with any inquiry. However, in taking on such a task, the leader is not doing the things that only he/she can do. Leaders of any creative endeavor should focus first on the things that *only they* can do—things that simply couldn't be delegated to others.

As the founder or originator of a creative pursuit, you may find yourself acting and thinking as the sole owner despite the presence of your team. But if you fail to share ownership, you'll also fail to get those around you to care. This is not about money; it's about mentality. Having only one person stay up at night thinking about how to solve a problem or capitalize on a particular opportunity is frankly not enough. You need to engage your team as owners by sharing credit, sharing responsibility, and sharing financial rewards.

Another common problem faced by once-solo leaders is the desire to have your team just get the job done rather than learn how to do the job better. Remember, however, that the people who work for you are likely interested in more than money; they want to become experts. Besides being the leader, you need to be a teacher. You will want to find opportunities to engage your team members in whatever interests them, even if it is beyond the scope of their jobs.

No great creative project can thrive (or even survive) off the energy of one person. You must evolve along with the scope of your creative ideas in order to make them happen.

3 LEADERSHIP CAPABILITY

WE HAVE NOW covered the mechanics of organization and execution as well as the important role that community plays in making ideas happen. But in the end, the quality and scalability of your creative endeavors rely on your capacity to lead. Your ideas will thrive only if you manage them as a leader rather than as an independent creative visionary.

There is a great void of leadership in the creative world. Creative projects run amok and teams break down all the time as a result of misaligned incentives, poor team chemistry, and inconsistent management. Of course, many of the obstacles that arise when we must lead a team come from our natural tendencies. We fall short of fully empowering others because we don't want to compromise the quality (or control) of our ideas. We struggle to engage the right people and exercise sound judgment amidst the anxiety and emotion that we face when challenging the status quo. When we fail, we often miss the precious opportunity to seize the lessons and build our capacity.

Leadership development is experiential. Through trial and error, good times and bad, we gradually become better leaders—but only if we are self-aware enough to notice when and why we falter. In this section of the book, I present best practices of great creative leaders as points of reference for your own personal journey. While leadership capacity is only enhanced through raw experience, we must always question our assumptions and compare various methods and convictions to our own.

We will start by examining the system of rewards that govern creative pursuits. Long-term vision is not enough. As we find ways to keep ourselves motivated, we will be able to do the same for others—as evidenced by a number of prominent entrepreneurs and leaders such as Ji Lee, creative director at Google. We will then discuss the unique chemistry of creative pursuits and how leaders like Diego Rodriguez, senior partner at design consultancy IDEO, build and maintain productive teams. And finally, after much discussion on how we lead others, we will turn our focus inward. After all, some of the greatest obstacles we face in leadership lurk within us. The fortitude to learn from our experiences and take risks is a result of a very personal sense of self-awareness. As we seek to effectively lead others, we must become more effective leaders of ourselves.

THE REWARDS OVERHAUL

WE ALL HAVE visions for the future, and most of us would argue that our daily efforts are all in service of a passionate long-term pursuit. But in reality, how we spend our energy is greatly influenced by the short-term reward systems that permeate our lives. For most of us, the ideas we capture, the knowledge we choose to master, and the tasks we complete are heavily influenced by the demands of those around us—as well as our own thirst for swift gratification.

The German philosopher Friedrich Nietzsche once said that you must "make yourself become who you are." So it is with creative visionaries and the ability to make ideas happen. The drive to pursue long-term creative goals goes against the grain of the comfortable trickling stream of short-term rewards that are meant to sustain us and maintain the status quo. To push our ideas to fruition—time and time again—we must find ways to overpower our basic tendencies and nearsighted motivations.

Short-Circuiting the Rewards System

From a very early age, our formal education ingrains a short-term rewards system that hampers our ability to make ideas happen. We studied for tests in elementary school in the hope of getting an "A." A good grade would garner respect from our teachers and approval from our parents. Once a graded test was returned, there was seldom an incentive to review incorrect answers. After all, a new chapter had already started and another test—with another grade—was looming. We became strategic—sure to spend our energy only studying what we knew would be tested—with the short-term goal of getting a better grade.

As we entered the workforce, the good grade became the paycheck, the recognition, and the potential for a raise or bonus. When a project is handed to us with a clear objective and a clear payoff, it is easy to economize our energy. The rewards system of the traditional workplace keeps us on track, in line with deadlines from the higher-ups. If we adhere to it, the deeply embedded reward system of our adult lives is likely to keep us employed and secure within the status quo.

However, these tendencies become destructive as soon as we begin to pursue long-term goals or attempt something extraordinary. Mustering the stamina to pursue bold ideas against all odds—and building a system of incremental rewards to make this possible—is an exceedingly challenging task. Regardless of how spectacular our ideas may be, short-term rewards—our desire to keep our job, get recognition, or garner a raise—are constantly nagging us, vying for our attention and enticing us to channel our energy elsewhere.

As humans, we are motivated by novelty. This is what makes the honeymoon stage of any new idea the easy part. When our vision is fresh and new, we happily shun other concerns and commit ourselves to deeply contemplating a new idea. But when execution appears on the horizon—and the harsh realities of actually making ideas happen emerge—the novelty wears off and our commitment to the long-term vision quickly fades. Without any incremental rewards to keep us on track, we begin to question our progress and the potential for success.

To successfully lead your team (and yourself) through bold creative projects, you must find ways to re-engineer your reliance on traditional reward systems. Rather than fight your natural inclinations, you must short-circuit your focus on the short term. To accomplish this you must hold two competing concepts in mind at once:

Unplug from the traditional rewards system. As you shift your focus away from short-term rewards, you must be willing to go without "success" in the eyes of others. You must embrace a different set of values that may feel uncomfortable to you and may even appear rash or unwise to others. Some entrepreneurs I've met claim to gain confidence when traditional investors doubt their ideas. Such doubts boost their confidence that they are, in fact, innovating rather than simply replicating something commonplace.

While it can be psychologically and financially difficult to depart from the race toward conventional rewards after a lifetime working with one mind-set, doing so is imperative to succeeding in the long term. Otherwise, you will struggle to sustain your long-term projects amidst the desire to be validated in the near term.

Stay engaged by setting up a system of incremental rewards. While it would be nice to believe that you can stay motivated to go against the grain based on willpower alone, you'll likely need an extra push. To achieve the sustained effort required to pursue spectacular achievements, you must trick yourself into staying engaged. If you cannot completely overcome your obsession with short-term rewards, you must use it to your advantage by establishing a regimented series of near-term rewards—the psychological equivalent of grades, paychecks, and affirmations. Whether it means prizing the value of lessons learned, building games into your creative process, or getting gifts upon certain milestones of achievement, self-derived rewards make a big difference. One entrepreneur I interviewed cited the growing number of results from a Google search for his company's name as a daily reward that his company sought for short-term encouragement. You must be creative in developing a set of incremental rewards that represent progress in long-term pursuits.

You cannot ignore or completely escape the deeply ingrained short-term reward system within you. But you can become aware of what really motivates you and then tweak your incentives to sustain your long-term pursuits. We'll examine some ways to mine alternative forms of compensation in the next few sections.

Happiness is its own reward. If you use the Internet and you wear shoes, chances are you've heard of Zappos.com. Zappos was founded in the dot-com heyday and has grown into the largest online shoe store. The company places a near-fanatical emphasis on service. Its success is largely attributed to its corporate culture, a facet of the company that earned it the twenty-third spot on *Fortune*'s 2009 list of "100 Best Companies to Work For."

"Powered by Service" is the Zappos motto, and when I visited the company's offices in Las Vegas, Nevada, my tour guide made the company's commitment clear. "Our product is customer service," he proclaimed. "We are a service company that happens to be selling shoes. Our next product could be anything . . . perhaps even an airline."

For a business that puts customer service at the center of its mission, the commitment and contentment of its employees is extremely important—and employee morale at Zappos is legendary. I was struck by the expression of company spirit as my tour guide led me through the company's cavernous hallways. Every department offered a custom greeting as we passed. The "Kids' Shoes" team shook their pompoms. The "Clothing" department rang cowbells. The "Company Coach," Vik, took a photo of me wearing a crown and placed it on the VIP wall—reserved for everyone who comes to visit Zappos. Because, Vik explained, "at a company all about service, everyone is a VIP."

The CEO of Zappos, Tony Hsieh, also serves as the company's cultural attaché, with a steady stream of speaking engagements, blog posts, and Twitter commentary. Hsieh believes wholeheartedly in the value of happiness as the backbone of a service-based business. Happiness, it seems, can even serve as an alternate form of compensation.

Employees don't often quit Zappos. And if they do leave, it is likely that they were paid to do so. Zappos provides a lump sum payment to any new hire who is willing to quit before the end of the training period. Part of the reason is that if you aren't really happy to be working at Zappos, it's likely to be reflected in the service you provide to customers.

The same principle guides the company's training programs, internal recognition award programs, and other perks; all initiatives are designed to foster happiness—not the ephemeral sense of happiness that comes from a midday game of Ping-Pong, but a deep satisfaction that comes from making progress in your life and being celebrated for your achievements.

Conspicuously absent at Zappos is an equity compensation plan or a revenue-sharing bonus structure for employees. While most entrepreneurial companies try to foster a sense of shared ownership among employees through stock plans and intricate incentive plans, Hsieh believes the answer lies in creating a sustainable culture.

"Most companies think that the number one motivator for employees is pay," explains Hsieh. "But if you ask our employees, I think it's number four or five, and above that are things related to culture or your manager or vocation and believing in the company's mission or vision. . . . This is one of the advantages we got from moving out of Silicon Valley where the mentality is very much 'I'm going to work four years, and then retire a millionaire.' . . . I think what we have here are people that truly believe in our long-term vision and also really feel like this is not just a job. . . . At the end of the day, it really comes down to what we are trying to maximize for employees, and [at Zappos] we are trying to maximize happiness as opposed to dollars."

At Zappos, happiness serves as a form of compensation without limits or tangible costs. Not only is it a core value of the culture, but it frees up financial resources that can be used in other ways—perhaps to lower prices for customers or pay for free overnight shipping. Happiness is the company's most valuable currency.

As you push ideas forward, you should make use of alternative rewards that keep you—and your team—engaged with your long-term pursuits. The traditional methods for acknowledging progress—financial rewards and celebrity among them—are unlikely to be available to you in the early stages of making ideas happen. Putting an emphasis on happiness changes the types of goals you pursue as well as how you hire and manage people along the way.

The Motivational Reward of Play

When Condé Nast's *Portfolio* magazine published its "Wall Street Is Dead" issue in late 2008, the photo editors were faced with a major challenge: the cover. Every mainstream newspaper and magazine around the world was talking about the tanking economy and the rampant fraud and recklessness on Wall Street. The well of ideas for visually presenting the economy was running dry. In need of a fresh perspective, the editorial team turned to Ji Lee.

Ji Lee is a polymath of creative pursuits. As the creative director of Google's Creative Lab, he has developed and executed plans to promote products like Google Maps, the Chrome Web browser, and the Goollery (Google plus gallery) initiative, a Web site that collects and showcases some of the most creative Google-inspired projects by people around the world. Outside of his day job, the prolific Lee has also completed dozens of personal projects that span the worlds of guerrilla art, illustration, and advertising campaigns—all contagious designs that engage consumers and passersby alike.

Perhaps the most famous of Lee's creations is the Bubble Project, in which he placed blank thought-bubble stickers on advertisements on the streets of New York. As Lee explains, "The bubbles were left blank, inviting passersby to fill them in. The project instantly transformed the intrusive and dull corporate monologues into a public dialogue." Launched in 2002, the project quickly spread around the world as other "ad-busters" adopted Lee's playful method for provoking guerrilla commentary. Print and television journalists as well as bloggers took note of the project, and it was ultimately cataloged in an eponymous book.

A more recent venture of Lee's is the "WTC Logos Preservation Project," an attempt to capture photos of signage and products around New York City that still display the city's skyline in its pre-9/11 incarnation. Like the Bubble Project, the WTC endeavor has evolved into an open collaboration in which participants navigate the streets of New York with an ongoing challenge to find and capture an undiscovered logo from a previous era.

As for Condé Nast's brief for the "Wall Street Is Dead" cover, Lee imagined the death of the iconic bronze sculpture *Charging Bull* by

Arturo Di Modica located near the heart of Wall Street. His inspiration became a doctored photograph of the bull lying dead amidst the flurry of New York activity.

Lee is an especially prolific idea generator who consistently executes ideas in remarkable ways. Like most creative minds, Lee has tons of ideas, but when it comes to actualization, he consistently beats the odds. Lee's fundamental secret for staying loyal to projects both in and out of the office is incorporating "an element of fun." For the Bubble Project, the experiment was kept alive through a playful relationship with the mainstream news media, who were captivated by Lee's masked anonymity. With the WTC logos endeavor, the project became an ongoing game as Lee attempted to find at least one old NYC skyline logo every day. "Games," Lee explains, "keep things simple and keep people engaged."

While play is useful for keeping oneself motivated, it's also a crucial tool for leaders. Both at Google and with his students at the School of Visual Arts, where he teaches regular classes, Lee uses games to foster learning, creativity, and motivation. One game he plays with his students and colleagues throughout the day involves an ongoing e-mail exchange of links—little findings that stretch the mind in some way. The game is the hot pursuit of the most clever and engaging or surprising link. The process is both playful and deliberate. "It's really fun, but at the same time it's very important, because I think it breaks the routine of their work flow and brings their brains to something totally different," Lee explains. "That's how creativity usually works."

To stay engaged, Lee advocates an overall balance in the types of projects he takes on. "Living at either end of the spectrum—spending your energy exclusively on all personal projects or all professional projects—will make you either poor or jaded," he explains. Instead, Lee is always working on multiple projects at the same time—up to four projects at work and six that are personal. From the outset, Lee searches for the element of fun and then makes it central to the project overall. The mediums he uses, the titles he selects, and the other people he engages all play into the element of fun that keeps the project sticky.

As you lead creative pursuits, find ways to incorporate elements of fun that keep you and your team motivated and engaged over time. Every creative effort has a project plateau where momentum is most often lost. Just as Tony Hsieh uses happiness as a form of engagement, Ji Lee finds and amplifies the fun and gamelike components of every project as a mechanism for short-term rewards. By placing a value on play and enjoyment, Lee is able to consistently conceive ideas and stay engaged long enough to follow through. The innate human desire for amusement is a powerful force that you should use to foster commitment and progress.

The Reward of Recognition

In a field that is particularly notorious for hoarding ownership and credit for ideas at the top of the organization, Joshua Prince-Ramus, president of REX, is an architect with something entirely different in mind. Upon the debut of his firm's first large-scale project, the Dee and Charles Wyly Theatre in Dallas, people gathered at the Wyly largely expecting a momentous announcement that would place Prince-Ramus in the spotlight as a hot, emerging architect. Instead, he went onstage with a different kind of message: "We, not me."

According to an article in *Fast Company*, Prince-Ramus went on to say, "The genius sketch is a myth. Architecture is made by a team of committed people who work together. . . . Success usually has more to do with dumb determination than with genius." And Prince-Ramus was not just talking the talk. When one of the firm's clients printed a brochure that attributed the credit for a REX building to Prince-

Ramus, he demanded that the brochure be reprinted with an alpha-betical list of the architects who were involved with the project.

Prince-Ramus's "we"-oriented approach contrasts sharply with that of the typical credit-hoarding executive. Years ago, I had occasion to meet the head of marketing at a start-up that was encountering some early success. Thomas, as we'll call him, had helped lead a number of start-ups and had dealt with his share of ego-driven CEOs. "It is pretty predictable," he explained. "When ideas prove to be great, the CEO takes tremendous pride. When things are rough, it becomes a blame game." Then his demeanor stiffened a bit and he further qualified his statement: "We have a great CEO. A real creative guy. But he thrives on his success and only truly recognizes the role of our team when dealing with something that goes horribly wrong."

Thomas's story illustrates what happens in a more typical top-down environment where higher-ups hoard all of the credit. The recognition accorded for the completion of successful projects is most powerful when it's distributed. As we see with Prince-Ramus and many of the leaders I have interviewed, success is more than a personal reward for leaders; it is a valuable currency that can be distributed to the team. The only bank account that the shared credit depletes is the leader's ego.

Recognition is a powerful reward that, whether or not money is tight, can help further engage those who play a role in making your ideas happen.

THE CHEMISTRY OF
THE CREATIVE TEAM

TAKING RESPONSIBILITY FOR the chemistry of your team can be just as effective as retooling rewards for emboldening your creative pursuits. You are the steward of the chemistry in every project you lead, starting with who and how you hire. As you cultivate a productive work environment, you must strike a balance between flexibility and expectations, idea generation and execution, and helpful disagreements and consensus. Your team's chemistry is a reflection of your ability to strike a harmonious balance and constantly make small tweaks in the service of making ideas happen.

During my visit with Zappos CEO Tony Hsieh, it was clear that a potential employee's culture-fit and commitment to serving customers are as important as the technical skills required for the job. To demonstrate this core value, Hsieh tells the story about a key technical hire—a top executive—whom the company recruited and moved from Los Angeles to Zappos's headquarters in Las Vegas. Upon arriving to solve some critical technology challenges for the company, the new hire made it clear that he wasn't interested in doing any direct customer support. The company fired him, losing quite a bit of money in the process. The reason? Zappos considers interest in customer support as a basic expectation, a prime element of the company's DNA.

As you build a high-performing creative team, you will want to look beyond technical skills and develop a chemistry that will transform ideas into remarkable accomplishments.

Engage Initiators in Your Creative Pursuits

Building a team of enthusiastic and talented people is one of the greatest challenges for leaders. A resumé gives little indication of a candidate's true mettle. Rather than focusing exclusively on an individual's experience, truly effective managers instead measure a prospective employee's ability to take initiative.

People who jump into whatever interests them, even if sometimes prematurely, power productive teams. A tremendous amount of energy and endurance is required to make ideas happen. As we now know, simply being interested in new ideas is not sufficient. Those who consistently take initiative possess tenacity and a healthy degree of impatience with idleness.

Not surprisingly, the best indicator of future initiative is past initiative. For example, consider a candidate applying to join your team who led an astronomy club in college and later helped found a not-for-profit that introduces astronomy to inner-city youth. Regardless of the nonastronomical nature of your project, this candidate is likely to take initiative if you can inspire interest in your pursuit. I have come to call these people "Initiators" based on their tendency to attach themselves to an interest and then relentlessly push it forward.

Earlier we heard from Jon Ellenthal, the president of Walker Digital, the unique R&D intellectual property firm behind such innovations as Priceline.com and a number of other successful patented inventions. Ellenthal and his team pride themselves on hiring Initiators rather than superstars. "I always try to hire people with a high level of intrinsic motivation," Ellenthal explains. "I don't want to spend my time trying to get people to do something. Ideas never get made unless everyone makes it their business to do so." More than anything else, Ellenthal strives to unearth Initiators. "I recall the days when I was a resumé snob," he says. "[But now] I would trade experience for initiative and the raw desire to do stuff in a heartbeat."

As you assemble teams around creative projects, probe candidates for their true interests—whatever they may be—and then measure the extent to which the candidate has pursued those interests. Ask for specific examples and seek to understand the lapses of time between interest and action. When you stumble across an Initiator—someone who has passion, generates ideas, and tends to take action—recognize your good fortune. Nothing will assist your ideas more than a team of people who possess real initiative.

Cultivate Complementary Skill Sets

Just as you should build a team of Initiators, you should also foster a chemistry of complementary expertise. Diego Rodriguez, a senior partner at IDEO, the design consultancy discussed earlier, cites the "T"—where the long horizontal line at the top of the letter represents an individual's breadth of experience, while the tall vertical line represents a depth of experience in one particular area. "At IDEO, we look to hire and build teams of 'T' people," Rodriguez explained to me. His expectation is that each person on a team should have both a general breadth of skills that supports collaboration and good chemistry and a deep expertise in a single area, such as graphic design, business, or electrical engineering. "The benefits of having 'T' people on a team is that everyone is able to relate across boundaries while also covering depth in one particular area."

Rodriguez attributes much of IDEO's success to a culture of mutual respect and a desire to be remarkable. The "T" concept enables teams to practice a true meritocracy in the process of idea generation. IDEO's use of rapid prototyping is all the more effective when people share enough broad knowledge and value for the culture that they can seriously consider solutions from their peers with a different area of expertise.

It is unlikely that IDEO has any greater understanding of electronics than Hewlett-Packard, or of banking than Bank of America (both IDEO clients). The expertise within IDEO likely exists within their clients' companies as well. It is the chemistry within teams at IDEO that makes all the difference.

When it comes to work flow and how teams are led, IDEO's chemistry is a competitive advantage. With careful hiring and a shared understanding, the various project teams at IDEO are spared from the clashes that are all too typical in other teams. Ideas can be pursued unencumbered by the misunderstandings and ego-driven antics that other cross-disciplinary teams must face daily.

Provide Flexibility for Productivity

As you develop some norms and expectations for your team's work flow, try to elevate true productivity over the appearance of hard work. Managers instinctively measure work ethic with an eye on the clock. Measuring work by time spent working is seductive, because it's easy and objective. But doing so defies the realities of the creative work flow and will ultimately damage morale.

In reality, ideas are made to happen in spurts.

The pressure of being required to sit at your desk until a certain time creates a factory-like culture that ignores a few basic laws of idea generation and human nature: (1) When the brain is tired, it doesn't work well, (2) Idea generation happens on its own terms, and (3) When you feel forced to execute beyond your capacity, you begin to hate what you are doing.

Rather than focusing on face time, creative teams should embrace transparency and strive to build a fundamental trust between colleagues. As leaders, we must create rules and norms for the sake of efficiency rather than as a result of mistrust. We should measure tangible outputs like actions taken and quality of outcomes.

Some companies have completely departed from the traditional mind-set that butts-in-chairs equals productivity. Best Buy, IBM, Sun Microsystems, and other major firms have implemented programs like ROWE (Results Only Work Environment), which measures performance based on output rather than *sit-put*. In a ROWE environment, employees are compensated based on their achievement of specified goals rather than on the number of hours worked. The ultimate goal is to empower employees to make their own decisions about when and where they work as long as mutually agreed-upon goals are achieved. This means that bosses stop watching employee calendars and paying attention to when people arrive and leave the office.

In one study conducted by Gallup Inc. reported in *Business Week*, productivity in departments at Best Buy that had adopted the ROWE program was up an average of 35 percent, along with a marked increase in employee satisfaction. It turns out that people thrive when their judgment and autonomy are respected.

Workplace flexibility can be a tricky conundrum—while it helps improve a team's chemistry, it also requires a certain degree of chemistry going in. There must be a shared level of trust and commitment to ensure that this autonomy is used for good purposes. More important, operating successfully in an autonomous environment requires that a concrete set of goals be established and constantly revisited. ROWE and other attempts at hands-off management fail miserably when objectives and goals are not mutually agreed upon and tightly managed. Many managers struggle to establish and repeatedly review goals with their teams. And, when a team falls short on goals, managers must confront it.

If you find yourself hesitant to support flexibility in your team, you should challenge yourself to find the root cause. Perhaps you're questioning your team's commitment to the projects. Or maybe the goals—or deliverables—are not specific enough. When leaders lack confidence in their team's preparedness and commitment, they compensate through increased control. Instead, you should examine the root cause. If you question your team's dedication, take a closer look at the chemistry. Are incentives aligned properly? Are their unaired doubts in the plan? Does each member of the team feel challenged, and fully empowered to do what he or she does best? Many small creative teams and start-up companies also suffer from unclear goals. A popular fix is to have regular ten-minute "standing meetings" at which the team reviews the current milestones and deadlines for progress. Another best practice is to have the list of major milestones up on the wall, visible to all. Just a quick check-in—or a glance up at the wall—can refocus an entire team on the priorities.

Admired leaders of creative projects are able to provide flexibility for their teams by keeping a close eye on the team's chemistry and ensuring that the priorities are clear to everyone. And when you feel the urge to question and control, seek out the root cause. Often, your own insecurity as a leader might prohibit you from providing the autonomy that your team needs to thrive.

Foster an Immune System That Kills Ideas

A strong chemistry in a team will not only support the development of new ideas but also help get rid of bad ones. In our bodies, the immune system plays the crucial role of killing off harmful viruses and bacteria. Without our immune system, our organs would fail from the constant invasion of new pathogens. Similarly, our ongoing projects face grave risks when new ideas arise during our process. Our ability to extinguish new ideas is critical to productivity and to our capacity to scale existing projects. In a team setting, the skeptics—the ones who always question ideas first rather than falling in love with them—are the white blood cells. The skeptics keep us functioning and help us stay on track.

While our natural tendency may be to not hire, engage with, or empower those with an inclination to poke holes in our ideas, these people are in fact essential to a productive creative environment. As Michael Crooke, president and CEO of outdoor apparel company Patagonia, proudly proclaimed at a Wharton West conference, "The people closest to me are all naysayers."

As you cultivate your team's immune system, you will want to differentiate between skeptics and cynics. Cynics cling to their doubts and are often unwilling to move away from their convictions. By contrast, skeptics are willing to embrace something new—they are just wary and critical at first. Though they are often undervalued, skeptics are an essential component of a healthy team, and leaders should cultivate their respect and influence.

Of course, there will be times when you will want to suppress the immune system and help the team play with ideas in an open-minded, blue-sky format—without skepticism. On such occasions, the skeptical members of the team should know their role and tailor their feedback accordingly.

The great challenge is to balance idea generation and relentless focus. While you don't want to behave like a large company that locks down all creativity from the point of production, you also don't want to act like a fledgling start-up that is always generating new ideas and features that saturate the project, ultimately getting in the way of execution. Finding the right balance requires allocating time for open idea exchange along with a healthy level of intolerance for idea generation during execution. One approach is to have a bias toward considering ideas during brainstorming sessions and killing ideas when they come up randomly during execution. Your resident skeptics can be helpful on this front. Of course, great ideas may still crop up unexpectedly, but when they do your bias should be to stay focused on the project at hand. With this approach, only the mightiest of ideas—those worthy of deep consideration—will risk getting you off track.

Fight Your Way to Breakthroughs

Conflict is a common occurrence in any creative process. It is a good sign, a powerful opportunity to refine your ideas and processes. Despite the frustration that friction causes, it will serve you in the long run if you are able to manage it. The leaders of great creative teams value the friction that results when opinions vary among a passionate group of creative minds. If good chemistry has been cultivated, teams can use disagreements to foster valuable insights that would otherwise be inaccessible.

Yet despite the opportunities that conflict provides, our tendency is to shy away from it. We will often completely disengage when a creative process becomes heated.

Conflict happens very easily. For any problem, there are multiple possible solutions—some better than others. In a diverse team, there will be many different opinions. Often, the person with the most power or experience just makes the call. Or sometimes people will openly disagree but eventually withdraw as the fight ensues. Conflict is a by-product of different viewpoints, but you cannot let it become a source of apathy.

Fighting is uncomfortable, but consider the benefits of opposing perspectives duking it out. Imagine that the answer to a problem lies somewhere on a spectrum between A and B. The more arguing that takes place about both ends of the spectrum, the more likely it is that the complete terrain of possibilities will be adequately explored. By contrast, if the advocates for A just give up, then B becomes the default answer without any better solution being discovered in between.

The alternative to healthy disagreement is apathy, a toxic state of mind that only encourages inertia. It is critical that you actively combat the tendency of some team members to withdraw from the dialogue when sparks start to fly—even if it means pulling colleagues aside and encouraging them to stick with it. The more individuals involved as the team triangulates on the solution, the better.

The best answer to any problem often dwells in the land of the unknown. If the members of your team have the fortitude to advocate for their perspectives while respectfully considering those of others, then the breakthrough will reveal itself. A leader's role is to keep people engaged in the debate and ruthlessly attack apathy.

As the leader of a creative team, try to foster healthy debate between people with different levels of influence and experience. One helpful practice is to get everyone to share proposed solutions or ideas first, prior to having people react. Junior people go first, followed by alternative proposals from the more experienced members of the team. Then, as people share their reactions, be sure that all members of the team stay engaged throughout the exchange. When you notice shortness or impatience, confront it with a question about process—something along the lines of "How can we keep all options on the table?" or "Since we're all trying to find the best solution, why are we getting impatient with each other?"

Some of the most admired creative teams share a common tenet— they are comfortable fighting out their disagreements and diverse points of view, but they always share conviction after the meeting. These teams recognize that the purpose of disagreement is to more fully explore the options. Fighting, as it turns out, is an asset for the teams that can stomach it. But the animosity is released when the exercise is over. Your team is more likely to conceive breakthroughs if its chemistry is strong enough to capitalize on conflict.

Don't Become Burdened by Consensus

As we debate solutions until we agree, we must also be sure not to become burdened by consensus. The ultimate challenge in collaborative projects is understanding how to draw on the best input of all without settling on the lowest common denominator. Consensus can often lead to a lackluster outcome.

To truly distinguish yourself as a creative leader, you must be able to gracefully incorporate a broad spectrum of ideas from the team and constituents of a project while still preserving the core mission.

Over the course of his career, Tom Hennes, founder of Thinc Design (mentioned earlier), has collaborated with an eclectic range of clients and partners on challenging projects, including California's Steinhart Aquarium, Freedom Park in Pretoria, South Africa, and the forthcoming National September 11 Memorial Museum. Each of these landmark projects was commissioned and managed by multiple stakeholders—the government, educational institutions, not-for-profits, donors, historians, and the general public—each with its own agenda.

Acting as an advisory and planning partner for Freedom Park in

South Africa was one of Thinc's most challenging projects. Both a memorial and a museum, Freedom Park is a national heritage site dedicated to telling the stories of those who lost their lives in the struggle for freedom in South Africa. The project revolved around the identity of an entire nation, and many, many different points of view had to be considered.

"Over twenty constituencies had a point of view," Hennes recounts. "The government, the historians, the spiritual populations, and many factions of the general public . . . each of which needed to be listened to and understood. We listened to the stories, to the struggles, and we listened deeply to their anxieties." Ultimately, Hennes and the Thinc team spent almost two years listening.

As Hennes described his approach to the project, I imagined the meetings he must have attended throughout the process. Planning a monument to a tragic struggle, a nation's progress, and lingering inequalities is only further complicated when everyone starts to provide their strong and likely emotional opinions. "Our job as designers," Hennes explained, "is to listen to what people are saying and then bring our skills to bear."

When working with an extended team of stakeholders, Hennes believes that his job is to listen to the stories, gather knowledge about all of the viewpoints, and then identify what he calls the "extremes" that will differentiate the project. Of all the ideas that his team comes up with, Hennes tries to find the few critical extremes that he wants to hold on to, and then commits to compromising on much of the rest. Hennes explained to me that the extremes are the ideas that he feels will most distinguish the end result. As he endures the inevitable battery of critiques and requests for alterations to his plans for a project, he holds these extremes sacred.

While most people might feel that incorporating two extremely different viewpoints (or features) into a project would call for an "either/or" decision that dispenses with one extreme, Hennes believes that consensus can often be achieved by taking an "and/and" approach.

One example Hennes cites is his collaboration with famed architect Renzo Piano on the Steinhart Aquarium project for the California Academy of Sciences. Initially, Hennes and Piano were at loggerheads—both wanted to achieve seemingly contradictory ends. While Hennes envisioned the aquarium as a dynamic exploratory landscape filled with nooks and crannies, Piano saw a rectilinear space with unbroken sight lines and clean architectural lines. The and/and solution was what Hennes describes as "a series of wild aspects that sit comfortably within a clean, linear architecture." It was a difficult problem to solve at first, but ultimately Thinc arrived at a solution that preserved the extremes and satisfied multiple constituencies.

Teams should not strive for complete consensus at the outset of a project. After all, consensus-driven teams run the risk of settling on what offends no one and satisfies no one. Early and complete consensus is comfortable but almost always unremarkable. Leaders of creative teams should identify and highlight the noteworthy, memorable solutions at both ends of the spectrum that, in all likelihood, are not agreeable to all. Over the course of discussions, they should seek to identify the few of these outliers worth fighting for amidst the other inevitable compromises when dealing with other constituencies. These *sacred extremes* are the ideas that you want to hold on to amidst all of the other compromises you will need to make.

Sometimes someone with a particular expertise should be empowered to vouch for the sacred extremes and make the final decision despite an uncertain team. We should be open to trying something new, especially when someone we respect is advocating for it. At Behance we empower the department heads to make the final decisions in their domains. For example, while everyone is empowered to question a design decision, our chief of design ultimately makes the final call. As we debate a solution, our chief of design will often compromise on a few details but insist strongly on any elements that he deems truly distinguishing (and thus sacred). On these sacred extremes, he will make the case for why they are crucial.

When it comes to making decisions, we should listen to all constituencies without feeling the burden to reach complete consensus. Ultimately, we must preserve the extremes and seek common ground on the rest. Otherwise, we risk mediocre creations.

In many creative teams, especially in the creative agency world, I observed an "input by many, decisions by few" strategy. Leaders would engage opinions broadly, then make final decisions in small groups. The notion of creative autonomy no longer calls for blocking out the opinions of the masses. Choose a process that engages all while preserving the extremes that make an idea extraordinary.

MANAGING THE CREATIVE TEAM

Leadership is the art of getting someone else to do something you want done because he wants to do it.

—President Dwight D. Eisenhower

CREATIVE JOURNEYS ALL begin with a spark in one person's mind. From day one, the challenge is to get others to understand and support the idea as though it were their own. But leadership is not about making people do things. Leadership is about instilling a genuine desire in the hearts and minds of others to take ownership of their work on a project. Only then can we act together, motivated by a shared purpose.

Sound leadership in the creative world is all too rare. Creative minds flee their teams at an alarming rate, and attrition is a common challenge. And when creative people do leave, it is seldom for a higher salary. Complaints from creatives who feel that their ideas are underutilized (or unheard) abound, as do stories of micromanaging leaders who demand that everything be done their way.

Across industries, I have found much in common among creative leaders who are able to consistently motivate a team to push ideas to fruition. These admired leaders are able to share ownership of their ideas, operate amidst adversity, and identify and develop high-potential team members. Through your own experiences managing others or being managed, you must develop your capacity to manage a creative team through the long, challenging pursuit to make ideas happen.

Share Ownership of Your Ideas

The more people who lie awake in bed thinking about your idea, the better. But people only obsess about ideas when they feel a sense of ownership. Alas, sharing ownership is easier said than done. More frequently than not, creative leaders struggle to surrender enough control over their ideas to truly allow their employees, partners, and other constituents to feel ownership.

Author and *Wired* editor in chief Chris Anderson, mentioned earlier, is a big proponent of sharing ownership of ideas. In fact, Anderson gauges the worth of an idea on whether or not anyone else is enthusiastic about owning it.

"When I have ideas within the magazine, I don't say, 'You, you, and you, act on this idea,'" he explains. "What I do is I say, 'Here's an idea. Who's interested?' And, you know, I articulate it to the best of my ability and I evangelize and I get people all enthusiastic and do as good a selling job as I can, and very quickly people might say, 'Man, that's exactly what I was thinking about!' . . . Or they're like 'meh' and in those cases I drop it. I don't push it through."

Getting people excited about your idea, however, is just the first phase of sharing ownership. The second and much more challenging part is empowering team members to push the idea forward rather than micromanaging them every step of the way.

Ultimately, truly sharing ownership of ideas means permitting your team members, the people you have entrusted with the fate of the project, to make meaningful decisions—even decisions that you might have made differently. The best creative leaders are able to recognize that the cost of variation from their original vision is often outweighed by the benefits of shared ownership and the scalability that it provides. You want your collaborators to stay up at night thinking about how to execute the ideas at hand—in their own way.

One seasoned creative leader who understands shared ownership of ideas is Peter Rojas. Originally the editorial director of the technology blog Gizmodo, Rojas went on to cofound the hugely popular tech/gadget site Engadget and become the chief strategy officer for Weblogs, Inc. In 2007, Rojas cofounded RCRD LBL, a forward-thinking online record label and blog, which became profitable after just fourteen months.

During our conversation, Rojas expressed his approach to shared ownership as largely pragmatic. "Leaders tend to want to put their hands on everything—but it is not productive [to do so]. . . . Engadget would have never functioned properly if I was that hands-on. . . . My approach is to hire people that I trust and let them do their thing. And if I don't trust them, I'll get someone else."

Trusting someone's judgment does not mean that everything is being done the way you would do it. Different people will make different decisions. The question, as Rojas points out, is: Did their alternate approach make a material difference? As long as the desired outcome is achieved, controlling how it is achieved shouldn't be that important to you.

The problem among especially passionate leaders is that their vision—and their obsession with perfection (or control)—often allows micromanagement to get the better of them. This happens for the best of reasons: We care deeply about both the process and the end product.

The problem is compounded for many leaders in the artistic sphere—such as fashion designers, architects, and photographers—

because their names are often part of the end product. Understandably, sharing ownership can become even more painful when your name and reputation are literally on the product.

However, the benefits of having your team feel collective ownership—waking with the impulse to improve the product and falling asleep generating new ideas to make the product succeed—will often outweigh the costs of having particular parts of the project develop differently than you may have intended.

Leaders Should Talk Last

Jack Welch, the legendary former CEO of General Electric, was known to walk into a boardroom full of his top deputies—all gathered to solve a problem—and proclaim, "Here's what I think we should do." Welch would explain his vision and reasoning. Then, after sharing his solution for the problem at hand, he would say, "Okay, now what do you think?" It is no surprise that Welch would get many nods of support and not much in the way of disagreement or bold, new ideas. Those who disagreed (and had the guts to say so) might share alternative ideas, but only in a context relative to what Welch had proposed.

Welch's good intentions were likely heartfelt. He was a seasoned executive with tremendous experience. However, even if he had the right solution in mind, he was still failing to fully engage—and develop—his team. And perhaps he didn't always have the right answer!

The tendency to talk first is a common flaw among visionary leaders. After many years in an industry, visionary leaders become revered by others and convince themselves that they have seen it all before. As a result, these leaders are liable to talk first, act quickly, and fail to engage others. When asked why they depart agencies, start-ups, and other creative teams midcareer, emerging creative minds often explain that they feel their ideas are not heard.

When we get passionate about our solutions, we tend to share them with excitement. However, when our responsibility is to engage the creativity of our colleagues, we must practice restraint. A creative team's purpose is to generate, refine, and execute ideas. If you fail to capture insights from each member of the team, then you are actually losing value.

The creative process is also a process of engagement. Enabling new or less-experienced members of your team to share their ideas is how you can develop their reasoning and bring them onboard. Instead of overshadowing their ideas with your own brilliant insights, silence yourself and welcome fresh, though sometimes naïve, insights. Challenge yourself to ask questions before making statements.

When you are not talking, you should be listening. Even those leaders who do recognize the value of talking last sometimes fail to listen while they are waiting to speak.

Judge and Be Judged Amidst Conflict

There is a saying: "You don't know who is swimming naked until the tide goes out." It is only when things go wrong that we are able to see what's truly going on beneath the surface. While conflict is never pleasant, as leaders we must acknowledge that conflict provides a precious opportunity to judge the leadership capability of others.

Admired leaders use conflict in two ways. The first is to evaluate the reasoning and patience of their partners or superiors. As soon as something goes wrong, they watch and learn. If you are ever unsure about the true chemistry and potential of a team, use conflict as an opportunity to measure it. Whether you are judging the leadership capability of your superiors, peers, or clients, performance during conflict is revealing.

The second way leaders use conflict is to build confidence and earn their team's respect. A number of accomplished CEOs, creative directors, and other leaders I have met attribute the greatest leaps in their careers to a crisis that they solved. It was less about the actual deal or decision that was made and more about the process of resolving conflict. They encouraged their teams to step back and regain perspective, to quit blaming and start brainstorming solutions. When their teams were plagued with doubt and uncertainty, these leaders seized the opportunity to combat apathy and rally their teams toward a solution. Naturally, amidst the anxieties associated with conflict, people are most impressionable when something goes wrong. Thoughtful leaders use conflict as an opportunity to align and strengthen their teams.

Develop Others Through the Power of Appreciation

In the autumn of 2005, I found myself driving from Boston's Logan Airport to a small town along the shore of Cape Cod to attend a storytelling workshop run by world-renowned storyteller Jay O'Callahan. One of my mentors at Goldman Sachs, Steffen Landauer, had recommended that I learn how to tell a decent story. "Leadership," Steffen would often say, "is most effective through the art of storytelling."

Without a doubt, Jay O'Callahan is one of the greatest storytellers in the world—a true master of his craft. One of the highlights of the workshop was just sitting back and listening to the man. With his wild, white hair, imposing stature, and carefully calculated delivery,

Jay was positively captivating. Not only a great storyteller, he was also a thoughtful and patient teacher.

Storytelling is a very sensitive form of artistic expression. The stories one shares are often deeply personal—attempts to make sense of childhood memories and reconcile our understanding of life's mysterious ways. For this reason, feedback on stories must be handled carefully. This was especially true for my storytelling workshop at "Alice's House" in Cape Cod. In a group of nine other students, I was the only participant under the age of seventy. While I had come to learn storytelling as part of my own professional development, I quickly realized that the other attendees had come for a different purpose. They were there to learn storytelling as a way to pass on their legacies, as stories, to their families. How do you critique one's telling of their life's story? While all creative projects are passion-driven and call for a delicate touch when it comes to feedback, storytelling lies at the far end of the spectrum.

O'Callahan would rely on the insights of those listening as he helped both experienced and aspiring storytellers hone their craft. Each participant would tell a story, and afterward the group would go around and share what O'Callahan referred to as "appreciations." The first story I told took place at college, during a moonlit walk through a graveyard with a few friends. I stood while recounting what I considered to be a mysterious and ultimately uplifting story about my friendship with two classmates. I tried to use my hands, because O'Callahan had commended the hand motions of the person who had spoken before me. I also tried to speak clearly and with whole sentences, often separated by a powerful pause—just as O'Callahan had done during his stories.

As I finished, O'Callahan clapped as his body rocked back and forth with laughter. "Wonderful, well done," he said. His enthusiasm and support, coupled with that of the group, was invigorating. For a moment, I thought that I had cracked the code of storytelling. Then

I remembered that I was an amateur, and I became eager to hear feedback. Had I spoken clearly enough? Was the plot at all confusing? Perhaps there was a portion of the story that could have been cut?

I was grateful for the positive response from the group, but I was eager (and somewhat anxious) for critical feedback. I wanted to know what went wrong. Then I remembered that the workshop operated with a very nontraditional approach to sharing feedback. Specifically, constructive feedback was not allowed. Rather than bracing myself for the onslaught of critical comments, I would have to refine my story by listening to the group's "appreciations."

Appreciations is a technique that O'Callahan and other storytellers use to improve students' skills without any demoralizing consequences. It's a unique form of feedback that helps creative professionals focus on developing their strengths. Here's the concept behind appreciations: having just shared a story (or, in other contexts, a presentation or idea), you go around and ask people to comment on the elements they most appreciated.

In my case, many people appreciated the pace at which I told the story. I also received a lot of unexpected comments about the character descriptions I had provided. After hearing the aspects of the story that people appreciated most, I got a sense for what strengths I should emphasize even more in future stories.

The exchange of appreciations is meant to help you build upon your strengths, with the underlying assumption that a creative craft is made extraordinary through developing your strengths rather than obsessing over your weaknesses. And I noticed that a natural recalibration happens when you commend someone's strengths: their weaknesses are lessened as their strengths are emphasized. As my storytelling compatriots recounted their stories a second and third time, the points of weakness withered away naturally as the most beautiful parts became stronger.

"It is strange that, in our culture, we are trained to look for weaknesses," O'Callahan explained to me. "When I work with people, they are often surprised when I point out the wonderful crucial details—the parts that are alive." O'Callahan went on to suggest that "if our eyes are always looking for weakness, we begin to lose the intuition to notice the beauty."

Of course, the contrarian's view to this approach is that more direct feedback and criticism might help one cut to the chase. O'Callahan would argue that appreciation-based feedback helps us access a deeper creativity:

> People need to relax to be able to discover. Our unconscious won't come forward and help us see things when we are too logical and focused on criticism. Sometimes someone will say, "I just want to know how to improve, not what is good." People think that pointing out faults is the only way to improve. Appreciations are not about being polite. They are about pointing out what is alive. The recipient must take it in, incorporate it.

The ability to recognize and share appreciations may, in fact, be more difficult than offering constructive criticism. Humankind is critical by nature. It is easier to hear an off note in a symphony than to identify the perfectly played note that makes all the difference. As O'Callahan explains, "Everyone thinks they can tell you what is good. But, no, it takes years to be able to say, 'That phrase is fresh, that was a lovely image, sheets on the bed like snow-covered mountains, lovely.' It is hard to get people to pay attention to that skill."

Of course, O'Callahan's approach to developing creative talent through appreciations applies to more than storytelling. Some creative teams incorporate elements of appreciation-based exchange in their review process. At one design firm I visited, a piece of work is placed on the table in a conference room, and everyone is asked to share three things they like about it. The artist takes away the feedback—all positive—and makes another version for the team to review. Almost always, the piece is dramatically improved. And the concerns that some members of the team had—but didn't share—are often minimized naturally. The team's morale and the general chemistry benefit from the exchange of positive encouragement, and the artist further develops his or her strengths.

Institute a round of appreciation-based refinement with your team prior to your formal process of critique. Your projects—and the skills of your colleagues—will be refined more organically by doing so. This change in the process of feedback exchange will not only improve output but also enrich the team's chemistry.

Seek the Hot Spots

Most companies place a great deal of emphasis on hierarchy, on who is in charge of whom. While the pecking order may affect salaries and titles on business cards, it is less relevant than you might expect when it comes to making ideas happen.

A study done in one large Fortune 500 company asked employees to complete a survey about who they go to for help. Whether it was a computer question, a finance inquiry, or something about the history of the business, employees were asked to provide the names of their "go-to" people.

Once the data points were collected, researchers mapped it out to graphically illustrate the flows of information. It quickly became clear that there were various particularly active "nodes" of information. Scattered throughout the organization, a handful of people functioned as the dominant go-to people who everyone else relied upon. Surprisingly, there was no correlation between the nodes and those with the most seniority or experience within the company.

One executive who looked at the data reportedly remarked on how scary it was to think that in a periodic round of layoffs the company could so easily lose critical nodes of information that it had never fully valued or formally accounted for.

The most successful leaders of change in organizations focus less on hierarchy and more on who has the best information. Ultimately, quality information leads to quality decisions. If you are able to identify the nodes of information in your organization, you will be able to lead with great understanding. We should all stop looking up and start looking around us for the people who seem to always know the answers.

Years ago, I had the opportunity to spend some time with Malcolm Gladwell as he spoke to a few groups of clients we had assembled at Goldman Sachs. He made a strong case that change doesn't always have to take time—that it can happen instantly—and that the catalyst behind instant change comes from what he called "social power."

Gladwell explained that social power is different than economic or political power. It is not correlated with status or demographics. Rather, people with social power have the special ability to connect to others en masse. They tend to always be in the know, and they are respected, although not necessarily in a hierarchical way.

My friend Erin Brannan, now a nonprofit executive, spent a few years in the Peace Corps stationed on the small island of St. Vincent, off the coast of Barbados. When I visited her there, I was struck by the unique impact she was having on the community. She explained to me that helping to develop schools or improve health care was nice, but lasting impact would come only from identifying and training those individuals who would perpetuate the good work for years to come. Over the course of our discussion, we coined the term "hot spots."

Whether on the island of St. Vincent or within a large organization, the hot spots are the people with social power. They are respected within the community without bearing the scrutiny that isolates and ultimately limits the potential of official leaders at the top of the hierarchy.

Hot spots are easy to identify if you ask the right people and look in the right places. Don't look for who gets the most credit or who is the most well-known. Instead, ask people where they go to get help. Seek out the people in your company or industry who are known for their reliability and uncanny ability to always know (or find) the answer. And then, when you identify the hot spots, listen to them and empower them. Give them more influence and responsibility. As you try to lead change through your creative endeavors, you should depend less on formal power plays and top-down transformations. Instead, you should seek out and engage the hot spots to ensure a lasting impact.

SELF-LEADERSHIP

THE MOST CHALLENGING one to manage is you.

"Self-leadership" isn't a concept that most of us think about all that often. Yet leadership capability relates as much to how we lead ourselves as to how we lead others. Some of the greatest barriers we face along the path to pushing our ideas to fruition lie within us.

Most creative leaders can trace their greatest obstacles to something personal—a fear, insecurity, or self-imposed limitation. As we consider past battles that drained our energy—such as a partnership that fizzled or a team that gradually disbanded under our watch—we must challenge ourselves to acknowledge our role in the failure. Our flawed judgment is often the root cause.

As you lead others in creative pursuits, you are your greatest liability. Self-leadership is about awareness, tolerance, and not letting your own natural tendencies limit your potential.

Find a Path to Self-Awareness

A motif throughout my research—and this book—has been the battle against our natural tendencies. The forces of organization, community, and leadership capability often evade us because our tendencies—to constantly generate more ideas, to isolate ourselves, and so on—get in the way. Even with insights and best practices for how to better generate ideas, organize projects, leverage communal forces, and lead others, it is still easy to regress.

Our best hope for staying on track is to notice when we stray and to figure out why—to be self-aware. Self-awareness is a critical skill in leadership, but it is deeply personal. It is not about our actions but about the emotions that trigger our actions.

Earlier we met Ji Lee, the überproductive visionary at the helm of the Google Creative Lab and a man with a long history of taking action on creative inspirations. When I spoke with Lee, he elaborated on the grander role of emotion in creative work. "Society teaches us to suppress emotions," Lee explains. "But, to effectively lead, you must understand and hone them."

Lee's personal journey, like that of many other leaders in the creative world, has included a commitment to psychological growth. For Lee, this meant group therapy. He describes group therapy as "all about being in the moment and really listening to others." In group therapy, members develop a contained set of relationships that play out much like the real world, but in a safe environment. The setting allows for self-discovery of the emotions behind your actions.

If someone says something that bothers you, you are encouraged to express that feeling. Statements like "What you said makes me angry," "You are annoying me," or "I feel afraid" are not uncommon. Expressing these raw emotions in a safe environment serves as a catalyst for understanding what lies beneath them. The insights gained from group discussion are especially empowering in the real world, where these emotions are almost always suppressed.

Lee and many other admired leaders in the creative world have made a personal investment—whether through group therapy, personal advisory boards, circles, or otherwise—to understand the emotional impetus for their actions. The construct of circles, discussed earlier, can serve as a source of self-awareness if members are willing to trust each other and feel vulnerable. Some other leaders I have met have assembled "personal advisory boards" for themselves—usually a group of three or four people with whom they share their fears and solicit candid feedback. The mechanism you choose can vary, as long as you are being challenged to be more introspective.

With increased self-awareness, we become better students of ourselves. When we make mistakes, we are able to identify what we could have done better more readily. When we receive feedback from others, it becomes more actionable as we come to understand its correlation with our emotions. The path to self-awareness never ends, but we must traverse it nonetheless.

Emerging leaders in the creative world benefit from some sort of psychological development in their lives. An early commitment to developing self-awareness will yield better judgment. In turn, sound judgment builds lasting relationships and great decisions—the kind that garner the respect and confidence you need to lead bold pursuits.

Develop a Tolerance for Ambiguity

With greater self-awareness comes a greater tolerance for uncertainty. Patience in the face of ambiguity helps us avoid brash decisions driven by our emotions instead of our intellects. We must use time to our advantage and temper our tendency to act too quickly.

The leader of a large technology company shared with me the challenges—and great bouts of anxiety—she faced when a large and well-funded competitor entered her space. The new competitor was willfully misleading her company's clients—claiming that her company's customer service was subpar and that their pricing was inferior.

But rather than rushing to draft a defensive marketing strategy and call customers, this leader stayed the course and introduced a new round of enhancements that trumped the competition. "I refused to let our momentary angst derail our well-thought-out plan," she explained to me. "As a leader, my job was to promote tolerance for a lot of crap in the meantime."

The best leaders have a high tolerance for ambiguity. They don't go nuts over the unknown, and they don't lose patience when dealing with disappointments. They are able to work with what they know, identify what they don't know, and make decisions accordingly. They also act with a faith in the law of averages. Over time, truth has a way of revealing itself.

A common occurrence in any organization is what I have come to call "momentary injustice." One of the most extraordinary leaders I worked with while at Goldman Sachs was then vice chairman Rob Kaplan. "Justice prevails over time in any good organization," he would say. "But justice does not prevail at any given point in time." A good leader, Kaplan believed, was able to overlook missed credit or an unfair project assignment by having faith in the course of an organization's growth.

There are laws of economics and human behavior that, over time, bring clarity and fairness to any situation. But impatient and impulsive leaders are liable to stumble during short-term periods of ambiguity. Their judgment becomes shaky and they can lose their grounding and respect within an organization.

The best practice here is to develop a tolerance for momentary injustice and periods of ambiguity. Stay strong and stay calm as a situation settles itself over time and the clouds around any period of change start to dissipate. Your fortitude will yield greater respect and opportunity that will reward you over time.

Capture the Benefits of Failure

When a project goes awry, we must remain open to the lessons that can be learned. As British author A. A. Milne once said, "Good judgment comes from experience, and experience—well, that comes from poor judgment." Digesting the realizations that accompany failure is a crucial part of the creative process.

Most of us have a hard time with failure because we feel not only the professional loss but also the personal hurt when our idea fails to gain traction. But this tendency poses a grave problem as we commit ourselves to act without conviction and kill ideas liberally. By doing so, we will meet many dead ends. Projects that encounter, or end with, failure have great value, but only if we can recognize it and reap the benefits.

When something goes wrong, there are three questions we should seek to answer:

What external conditions may explain the failure? When the outcome of any creative project is not what you intended, you should try to identify what, if any, external factors were responsible. Perhaps the client's brief was not properly explained, or the timing was wrong.

Perhaps there were other signs that the support required from others was missing. There are lessons to be learned that will help you better steward future projects.

What internal factors may have compromised your judgment? When a project falls short of expectations, there is almost always something that you could have done differently along the way. Perhaps you didn't seek enough restraints from the client. Maybe there were incorrect assumptions that you made in the early stages of the project. Ask yourself: if you had to pick two things that you would have done differently, what would they be? You don't need to share your answer with others, but you should challenge yourself to have an answer. Through self-awareness, you should be able to identify the factors that compromised your judgment.

Are there any gems in the unintended outcome? Francis Ford Coppola once quipped, "Art is partly being available to accidents that fall into your lap." Achieving this sense of availability can be especially difficult when your flow is disrupted by the unexpected. But rather than dwell only on what went wrong, consider what you may have inadvertently discovered.

Avoid the Trap of Visionary's Narcissism

During my time at Goldman Sachs, I had the opportunity to be a fly on the wall in a lot of meetings in the executive office during both the dot-com bubble and the dire period that followed it. I always found it interesting how every challenge was presented as an unusual one-off: "Never before have we had a market bubble, followed by such volatility in interest rates, interspersed with terrorist concerns."

The business leaders would nod their heads in affirmation. "This is an extraordinary time," someone else would say.

Based on all the times I have heard "This is the most unusual X, the greatest period of Y, the new era of Z," you might think that had I not been born in the last thirty years I might have missed the most exciting years of business since the beginning of time! Of course, if you consider the big picture, you see more patterns than exceptions. There was the railroad craze, the tulip craze, the radio craze, the Internet craze—and the leaders who bought in, the "carpe diem" executives who put it all on the line each time.

Nevertheless, despite history, the tendency to think that a given opportunity or challenge is a one-off persists. I have come to call this propensity "visionary's narcissism"—it is a leader's default thinking that he or she is the exception to the rule.

As creative minds, we are especially susceptible to bouts of visionary's narcissism. Not only can we get carried away with the uniqueness of a particular problem or opportunity, we crave firsts and love to do things differently. While our tendency is to approach every creative project with a fresh set of eyes, we should also accept a grounding realization: not much is entirely new, and yes, we can adequately learn from the past.

Challenge yourself to have some perspective. Don't get so caught up in the novelty of what you are doing that you lose touch with what's been done before. As you encounter negotiations with clients, collaborations with vendors and partners, or unique decisions or investment opportunities in your business, ground yourself with the fact that the situation you face isn't as isolated and unique as you think. Previous knowledge is yours for the taking, often risk-free and time-tested. Today never feels like it will be history, but it will. And more likely than not, you will look back and realize that you should have known.

Combating Conventional Wisdom with Contrarianism

As you harness the lessons of the past, you must also question them. Of course, nobody should willfully disregard good advice and fall victim to visionary's narcissism. But as creative professionals, we cannot become imprisoned by the status quo.

Yet another conundrum arises: how should we reconcile our tendency to seek the advice of experts with our desire to do things differently—and perhaps better? We should be wary that "best practices"—the tried and true ways of doing things—often become conventional wisdom, and conventional wisdom is often wrong.

There is a somewhat healthy tendency in every discipline to defer to the knowledge of elders. From the apprenticeships of the pre–Industrial Age to the traditional corporate hierarchies that permeate our life today, societies are built on collective wisdom from the past. Major conferences around the world gather industry experts to share their wisdom. We painstakingly listen to our elders' projections as if they were coming from an oracle.

However, for the small portion of society that is tasked with innovation and pushing the envelope, a reliance on conventional wisdom is damning. We have to temper advice with a dose of skepticism, and we must always consider the merits of developing new platforms rather than more and more derivatives.

An early theme that emerged in my interviews with creative professionals was the practice of "contrarianism," or the act of purposely thinking against the grain when approaching problems and brainstorming new ideas. Contrarians are willing to manage (if not embrace) the uncertainties and risks inherent in thinking differently. And by questioning the norms, they are bound to either find better approaches or to feel more confidence in the old ways of doing things.

The following are a few tips for engaging in the practice of contrarianism and navigating the terrain of conventional wisdom. Need-less to say, consider them with a dose of skepticism!

Don't revere someone based on age. There is an inherent preju-dice against young people—or people who are new to our industries—because we question how much they could possibly know given their relative lack of experience. However, novices have very legitimate ad-vantages when it comes to detecting trends, adopting new technology, and attempting risky undertakings that more experienced creatives would shy away from. When working with novices, you should pass judgment on their raw interests and skills rather than their age or number of years in the industry.

Reconsider your approach to mentoring. Your tendency may be to look to those above you for guidance, connections, and opportuni-ties. Yet your greatest advisers, partners, colleagues, and financiers are likely sitting around you rather than standing in front of you at the podium. While society may suggest that you have the most to learn from those at the top, you must make an effort to look around and below you as well. View mentoring less as an act of graciousness and more as a strategy to capture the benefits—through relationships or otherwise—that are likely to transpire for you as well.

Distinguish past accomplishments from present knowledge. We all have a tendency to "rest on our laurels," but cutting-edge knowledge becomes antiquated very quickly. The brilliant expert from yesterday may have little insight that is relevant today. In fact, such experts may be too biased by their own past experiences and success to see how the times have changed. As such, you should ques-tion the correlation between one's past accomplishments and present knowledge.

Aspire to better practices, not the best. Rather than default to the way things have already been done, recognize that anything can be done better. While it is certainly worthy to find and follow time-tested methods as we pursue projects, it is dangerous to passively accept advice. All conventional wisdom and "best practices" should be taken with a grain of salt and built upon as we aspire to "better practices." (This applies just as much to the advice in this book!)

Consider Yourself an Entrepreneur

You have a responsibility to make your ideas sustainable. For an idea to thrive over time, it must be treated as an enterprise. Whether you work in a large corporation or on your own, when it comes to leading ideas, ultimately you are an entrepreneur.

"Entrepreneurs are not the ones with the best ideas," says Andrew Weinreich, a trailblazing serial entrepreneur. "They're just the ones willing to jump off a cliff without the answers." Weinreich created one of the earliest social networks, SixDegrees.com, which he eventually sold in January 2000 for $125 million. Most recently, he has founded Xtify.com, which offers free location-based services for mobile phones and Web apps, and MeetMoi.com, a mobile dating service. In all of these ventures, Weinreich has played the role of founder and leader.

Weinreich's business escapades did not start with thoughtful strategy and business planning. He graduated from law school with over $100,000 in debt. But he had ideas and grand visions of what they might become. "You can live longer off passion than off money," Weinreich explains to me. But when he took the plunge on his first venture, he didn't see a finish line—and he thinks it is wrong to have one in mind. Instead, he believes that entrepreneurs should just try "to stay in the fifth inning forever"—meaning they should focus more on incremental progress than on the need to win. The big win is likely far off in the distance, many iterations and ideas away from the current state of the project. This practice of perseverance is consistent with the notion of short-circuiting your reward system. Weinreich calls it "the process of willful delusion." You must somehow stay engaged with incremental progress and maintain momentum, even if you find yourself staying in the same inning—making repeated attempts at the same idea.

"When our [start-up team] first came together," Weinreich recalled, "I told them that their biggest risk was joining the team—and that the rest of the experience would just be filling the holes in the boat. If we sat still, the boat would sink. The faster we moved, the more slowly the water would creep in, and we'd simply plug all of the holes over time." Weinreich believes that the key to surviving the start-up experience is momentum. "When you stop moving, the music stops."

For Peter Rojas, the cofounder and CEO of RCRD LBL, mentioned earlier, the hardest part of pursuing a new idea is "pulling the trigger—being mentally in it or out." He recalls that after he left Engadget he had a number of other tech-focused ideas regarding video networks and TV, but he decided that his mind wasn't fully engaged by any of these ideas. He wasn't ready to jump off the cliff.

When you come across ideas worthy of your time and energy, it is important to know which assurances you need—and which you don't—before you decide to take the plunge. You don't need (nor will you ever have) all the answers, but you do need to feel that the risk of giving it a go is less than the risk of not trying. You don't need to see a finish line in sight, but you do need enough momentum to stay afloat.

In Anne Lamott's international best seller *Bird by Bird*, about the art of writing, she cites a quote by the award-winning American author E. L. Doctorow on what it is like to write a novel. "It's like driving a car at night," Doctorow proclaims. "You never see further than your headlights, but you can make the whole trip that way."

Along the journey to turn ideas into action, you must keep up the momentum, even if you can only see a few yards ahead. Most entrepreneurs will admit that the value of having a masterful business plan is overrated. What matters most is your ability to keep moving and pushing your ideas forward, yard by yard.

Be Willing to Be a Deviant

We have talked a lot about the personal obstacles that are common in creative pursuits and how to overcome them. In addition to the challenges posed by our own tendencies, there are also external, often societal, pressures that, at weak moments, can obstruct our journey.

Most of the extraordinary creative minds I interviewed over the course of writing this book spoke of times in their lives when they made decisions that were unpopular but necessary. Whether it was dropping out of college to pursue a passion, quitting a well-paying job to start a company, or declining certain opportunities that appeared golden to others—their paths were unconventional. As these budding creative leaders hacked their own paths, they lost support from others. But amidst a cacophony of discouragement from teachers and even their own families and friends, they persevered and learned to gain confidence from being questioned. They became deviants of a sort.

Deviants are maverick-like, willing to be unpopular, misunderstood, and even shunned during creative pursuits. The vision of extraordinary achievement is, by definition, a few steps beyond consensus and conventional logic. As such, we should become emboldened by society's doubts rather than deterred.

Society is a bit hypocritical. The mainstream shuns wayward creative people with skepticism, especially when they defy the status quo. Dropping out of school or choosing an alternative career is frowned upon. But at the same time we celebrate the successes of the artists and entrepreneurs who enrich every aspect of our lives. Society celebrates the outcome of what society shuns.

We make grave errors when we consider creative success as a one-off. Ideas are not made to happen by accident or out of luck. Creative achievement is simply the logical outcome of doing something different and seeing it through to completion. What society views as a tremendous risk may appear to some of us as an obvious and compelling opportunity. Whether or not the project becomes something meaningful depends on our capacity to organize and lead.

You must learn to gain confidence when doubted by others. The uncharted path is the only road to something new. As pressures mount, you need to stay the course and consider the doubts of others as an indication of your progress.

You cannot rely on conventional knowledge, rewards, and procedures as you lead creative pursuits. As you have learned, the ways that you manage your energy and engage employees and partners must all be questioned. Nothing extraordinary is ever achieved through ordinary means. With a deviant mind-set, the pressures from others become a source of confidence. By shedding the obligations and expectations bestowed upon you by the status quo, you can organize and lead extraordinary ideas to fruition.

Keep an Eye on the Backward Clock

In hindsight, it is easy to talk about assuming the deviant mind-set and defying the status quo. But it is very difficult to take the leap. Many of us postpone our creative pursuits for a whole host of reasons. We want to stay in our current jobs a little while longer, perhaps to increase our savings or get "one more promotion." Or maybe we are "waiting for the right time" but can't really say for sure when that time will come. These might be rationalizations. Or, they might be perfectly good reasons to put off actualizing our ideas. Either way, we pay a price for postponing action.

Consider for a moment:

> You are sitting in a dull meeting. Tuning out the conversations, you become entranced by the passage of time on the wall clock. You watch sixty seconds pass, a minute of your life that you will never get back.
>
> During that time, were you taking any risks to push your ideas to fruition? Were you moving the ball forward in any way? Were you marketing yourself for an opportunity to get closer to your true interests—or angling to further develop an area of expertise? Were you harnessing the forces of connection and opportunity around you?

Depending on how you consider your current career and the state of your ideas, this vignette is either a painful reminder of wasted time and lost opportunity, or a motivational reminder to use every minute to pursue life to its fullest.

The notion of the backward clock is simple: if you were told the exact year, day, and time that your life would end, would you manage your time and energy any differently? Even if that date were seventy-three years, twelve days, two hours, and thirty seconds from now, would you become more aware of time passing, minute by minute?

In essence, we all have a final date and time ahead of us, but we are not burdened with a countdown. This is probably a good thing, given the anxiety that such information would create. Nevertheless, there are some benefits from keeping an eye on the backward clock. As you seek to capitalize on your creative energy, insights, and ideas, the window of opportunity is always closing. A dose of pressure is a good thing.

The fact that time is ticking should motivate you to take action on your ideas. When little opportunities present themselves, you might decide to seize them. An eye on the backward clock helps you stomach the risk because, after all, time is running out. Get on it.

The Love Conundrum

Love plays a strange role in creative pursuits. At first, love sparks our interest and a relentless desire to focus and learn. During the tough times and project plateaus, love keeps us engaged. But love also creates a chasm between our visions and accomplishments. Love can lead to great disappointment.

Love drives us. There is an extraordinary gentleman named Jason Randal who knows a lot about love. You may have seen Randal perform magic on one of the late-night talk shows or at world-famous conferences. Or perhaps you have seen his stunt double work in one of his films, including *An Officer and a Gentleman*, *Tequila Sunrise*, and *Pretty Woman*. Even if you have, you probably don't know that Randal holds a PhD in social psychology, plays and writes for five musical instruments, speaks three languages, and is a board-certified master hypnotherapist, licensed locksmith, NAUI master scuba instructor, and master certified flight instructor for both airplanes and helicopters.

We're not done. Randal is also a seventh-degree black belt in karate and has instructed for six years at the Chuck Norris karate school. Believe it or not, the list goes on. More than anything else, Randal is an expert in developing an expertise.

Lucky for all of us, Randal is willing to share his secrets. He emphasizes three critical components for developing a mastery: (1) a deep desire and interest in a topic, (2) the ability to learn it, and (3) the capacity to enlist support. The deep desire and interest, Randal explains, prompts an intense and lasting engagement with the topic. When you couple this obsession for a topic with the ability to learn (through comprehension, mnemonics, or otherwise) and the involvement of others, you can accomplish extraordinary feats.

As Randal describes his approach to his many interests, the common theme is a deep and authentic love for every skill he has developed and his experiences using them. Randal has an insatiable desire to become better, but not out of ambition or competitiveness. Randal is driven by love. Love keeps him engaged long enough to learn, experiment, and take bold risks. As a tremendous salesman of his own projects and philosophies, Randal is able to engage his community. His positive energy is contagious, and his projects benefit as a result. Randal demonstrates how love can carry us toward great accomplishments.

Love disappoints us. In the beginning of the book we met Jonathan Harris, a very accomplished artist whose projects are all complex attempts to explore his fascination with emotion. When I met Harris, he shared the complicated role that love plays in his work.

"The love you have for what you're doing is actually the most important thing," Harris explained. "Love is the only thing that's going to pull you through and get you to finish . . . but there is also a paradoxical and interesting fact: The thing you actually end up making is going to be such a failure compared to the original feeling that you had, the original vision that you had. If you finish and you find out that it's not a failure, it means that you didn't try hard enough, because when you really fall in love with something, you idealize it, and you develop a vision of it that's actually unattainable in reality. The feeling of it is so pure that you can't make a real thing that has that feeling and so you're inevitably going to be disappointed by it. And in some way, the depth of that disappointment is in direct correlation to how beautiful the vision was to begin with."

Harris argues that love motivates us, keeps us loyal throughout our projects, and then ensures some level of disappointment at the end.

Reconciling love. You may have heard the old quote "How do you get someone to stop enjoying what they love to do? Pay them to do it." The adage suggests that when your passion becomes your work, your relationship to your passion changes. There are many examples we've come across—a designer gets hired by a big firm, an entrepreneur gets hired to run a business within a large company, a novelist gets commissioned to do a story for someone else—in which a bout of suffering sets in as we start to go through the motions. The mechanics of these projects weigh on us. As we relinquish control and realize that others will take credit for the outcome of our labor of love, we start to question ourselves.

Your challenge is to maintain an organic relationship with the craft that you love. The expectations and rewards imposed by others will only compromise your passion if you rely on them as the source of your interests. Like a fleeting sense of lust, passion fueled by traditional incentives will quickly fade. You must stay focused on the intrinsic rewards of your work and stay motivated by the means rather than the ends.

Love is a cause of both commitment and then, often, a great deal of disappointment. But an enduring love for an idea or interest can push you past the obstacles. The people who transform industries and change the world are people who have mastered what they love. They continue to practice their craft because they love the process more than the outcome. And they are constantly finding new ways to reengage, keeping the love affair alive despite the suite of pressures that come between our visions and reality.

AFTERWORD
Optimizing Your Capacity
to Make Ideas Happen

I AM DEEPLY grateful for the feedback and inspiring stories people have shared with me after reading *Making Ideas Happen.* The book has provided me with the opportunity to travel the world and work with small teams and large companies across industries—with groups in government, as well as with large companies like General Electric, Procter & Gamble, and of course many small creative agencies, start-ups, and creative individuals. While our ideas vary widely, our struggles are very much the same.

In our constantly connected lives, we are all searching for ways to be more proactive in what matters most to us and less reactive to the cacophony of communication, information, and distraction that drains us. We all strive to better manage our energy, prioritize, and work with a bias-toward-action—but we're never quite good enough.

Whether we're working in a large company, a medium-sized business, or a start-up, we all fight against bureaucracy and battle the friction that makes it so difficult to push ideas to fruition. Even among the most productive people and teams I have met, these struggles never end.

In the years since the initial publication of *Making Ideas Happen*, I have realized that pushing great ideas to fruition is not just about shifting your mind-set, approach, and habits in the here and now. It also requires a continued dedication to optimization in the long term.

If you work in technology or web development, you've likely heard the term "optimization." It's the process of incrementally improving a product or service through small iterations. As anyone who manages an online business knows, launching a great Web site is just the beginning; constant tweaks and upgrades are required to create something truly extraordinary.

The same is true with regard to executing ideas of all kinds—not to mention growing as individuals and leaders. To truly excel, we must constantly be fine-tuning our approaches to making ideas happen on every level.

As you work to integrate the insights from this book into your personal and professional life, I would encourage you to keep two best practices of optimization in mind:

1. Make Incremental Tweaks, Not Drastic Changes

Optimization isn't about making drastic changes. The key to optimization is making incremental tweaks in a controlled and measurable way. Google is famous for its relentless "A/B testing," a form of optimization that involves making minor adjustments to their applications and then testing the newest version side by side with the previous versions. Using Google users as their testers, Google will run a "version A" (the current version) and "version B" (the experiment with minor tweaks) and then compare the results.

For example, version B might have a sign-up button moved one-tenth of an inch to the right, compared to version A. If version B garners 3 percent more clicks, then version B becomes the standard and replaces A, and then the process keeps repeating itself. By running isolated tests and measuring the outcome, Google is able to improve their products without the risk of damaging a successful business.

When you decide to tweak the way you take notes, run meetings, prioritize, or manage your team, try to introduce one factor at a time and identify how you will measure the impact before you start to test it. Just as you might run A/B tests on your products, services, and marketing efforts, you can also optimize your own workflow in the same way. Doing "A/Me" testing involves you comparing the way you always work "Me" to a slightly tweaked approach (the "A" in this case).

Perhaps you question the usefulness of checking your e-mail on your mobile phone as soon as you wake up every morning. Try shifting this habit for one week and wait to check your e-mail until you begin your commute or arrive at the office. Then, analyze how the week felt under this new discipline and decide whether or not to institute this change going forward.

2. Tinker with What Works

When you make a mistake, the natural instinct is to persevere and keep trying until you get it right. But when you get it right—when you hit a home run—the human tendency is to rejoice and then move on to the next challenge. Despite research that encourages us to build on our strengths, we spend more time fixing what's broken than optimizing what works. Why?

This is because any measure of success impairs our ability to imagine something better. I call this the "horizon of success" effect, because it's hard to see the potential that lies beyond something that works. While it seems logical to risk failure by trying something completely new, it's unsettling to tamper with a known success. The old adage "if it ain't broke, don't fix it" cripples us when it comes to optimizing what works. Yet, the very premise of optimization is that we must constantly fix what isn't broken.

Don't neglect your strengths and focus only on your weaknesses. On the contrary, efforts to optimize should be spent on your strengths. Small tweaks are the difference between 95 percent and 100 percent. If you can find your 95 percent and really bring it home, that's where you are most likely to change the world.

Optimization isn't about drastic change or self-help, and it isn't spiritual. It's all technique. You can't rest on your laurels. Despite the quality of your ideas and output, the impact you will make largely depends on your ability to constantly optimize—to build on your successes and grow them into something greater.

Here at Behance, we continue to focus on optimizing our own efforts to organize and empower creative people and teams to make ideas happen.

Since the publication of this book, 99U has grown to become a very popular annual conference and online think tank devoted to the execution of ideas. Behance has made great strides in helping organize the creative world's work and has since become a part of the Adobe family, now reaching millions of creative people and teams around the world.

We are deeply committed to this work, and we are honored to do it. Developing the capacity to push your ideas to fruition is a life-long pursuit for all of us. Stick with it.

Scott Belsky

AN OPPORTUNITY AND A RESPONSIBILITY

WHEN PEOPLE HEAR a new album, read a new novel, or celebrate the achievements of a revolutionary new product or business, they seldom grasp the magnitude of effort and capabilities required to create it. But as creators ourselves, we should view the world of innovation with a lens that sees beneath the glamour. We should round out our creative talents and impulses with a continuing education in the forces of execution.

The case studies surround us every day. When breakthroughs and accomplishments are celebrated—spectacular movies are released, novels are published, and companies grow—we should work backward in our minds and imagine all that was required to push the idea to fruition. How much organization and sheer perspiration was involved? How many late nights, team fights, and spurts of personal growth took place along the way? How many drops of perspiration (and tears) were shed?

There is a deep sense of understanding and respect shared among creative leaders who have encountered success. The bond is not a result of their shared sense of achievement. Rather, it is the result of empathy and mutual admiration. Regardless of industry, every creator who has successfully made an idea happen has fought and survived a very long war. While the scars and memories may be from different battles, they all know what it's like to be out there, struggling across the project plateau and constantly pursuing innovation against the grain.

Our raw curiosity and sense of wonderment fuels our ideas, but bringing them to fruition requires a steadfast commitment. All of the insights, unnatural restraints, and personal compromises we have discussed are part of this arduous commitment. And if you stick out the journey, you will have a unique opportunity to make an impact in your world.

It is not naïve or a cliché to say that the creative mind holds the answers to all of the world's problems. It is merely a fact. And so, you should balance your desire to use your creativity with a sense of responsibility.

Please take yourself and your creative pursuits seriously. Your ideas must be treated with respect because their importance truly does extend beyond your own interests. Every living person benefits from a world that is enriched with ideas made whole—ideas that are made to happen through your passion, commitment, self-awareness, and informed pursuit.

Challenge yourself to withstand the self-doubts and societal pressures that will rally against you. When they do, take comfort in the knowledge that you are in good company. We all struggle, but we persevere. Adversity makes us stronger. Relish the fact that you are on an important path, emboldened by both the opportunity and grave responsibility to create something of value—a value that is rewarding for you and enriching for all.

Acknowledgments

WHILE THIS WORK is the result of many years of research and writing, the idea would never have materialized without the support and leadership of my colleagues on the Behance team, mentors, and family. Many of the concepts and perspectives shared in this book are the result of your influence and the opportunities you have provided. While I have sought to cite every source properly, I know that my knowledge is an outcome of countless discussions, experiences, and great mentorship. I am extremely grateful and want to acknowledge the great impact you have had on this book.

Matias Corea, my founding partner and the chief designer of Behance, has taught me that design is at the center of organization and communication. His vision has enabled Behance to make an impact in the creative world, and his partnership has made all the difference along the way. I learn from Matias every day, and the research and realizations of Behance are an outcome of our friendship and his leadership and mastery of design. I also thank Matias for the art direction and design of the cover for this book.

I am extremely fortunate to work with a brilliant and committed team at Behance. David Stein, Chris Henry, and Bryan Latten have led technology at Behance since the early days. Their insights and stewardship of Behance extend well beyond our services and played a crucial role in our research. I also wish to thank Dmitry Traytel,

Jackie Balzer, and our growing technology team that has rounded out Behance's technology and development and have infused new insight into Behance's products and services. I also want to thank Alison Thornsberry, Behance's business manager, who has helped scale our team and support a culture that lets us practice what we preach.

I extend my gratitude to my colleagues Alex Krug, Oscar Ramos Orozco, Zach McCullough, Clément Faydi, Sarah Rapp, Mell Ravenel, Caitlin Strandberg, Malcolm Jones, and Will Allen for breathing fresh insight and leadership into Behance. As Behance's senior designer, Zach is also to thank for his help with the illustrations for this book. Behance would also not be what it is today without our special relationship with JB Osborne and Emily Heyward from Red Antler—and the guidance from our esteemed advisory board members. Thank you!

Jocelyn Glei started working with me in 2008 as a research assistant for this book and became the ultimate partner in editing and debating the merits of the tips and insights throughout the book. She also became the director and editor in chief of The 99%. Jocelyn is a brilliant journalist and writer in her own right. I am grateful for her commitment to and endless energy for this project—it would not have been possible without her.

Steve Kerr and Steffen Landauer were managers and mentors to me early in my career at Goldman Sachs. The opportunity to follow around and learn from Steve and Steffen was absolutely fundamental to my understanding of leadership development. By inviting me to join the Pine Street team, Steve and Steffen provided an experiential education beyond my wildest expectations.

I had the great fortune of being able to work with Professor Teresa Amabile during my second year at Harvard Business School. I am grateful for Teresa's willingness to serve as a mentor and adviser during my independent research.

As I reflect upon great mentors, teachers, and confidants who have provided advice and played a key role in this journey, I wish to thank Deborah Streeter, John Jaquette, Michael Schwalbe, Michael Brown, Itai Dinour, Quanda, Reboot, the LifeRemix folks, the team at TED, Evan Orensten and Josh Rubin at Cool Hunting, Sheila Danko, Aaron Dignan, Josh Spear, Charles Torres, and my good friend (and first partner in business), Ben Grossman.

My agent, Jim Levine, and my editor, David Moldawer, along with his team at the Portfolio imprint at Penguin, have provided invaluable guidance and support over the course of the project, for which I am extremely grateful.

I want to extend a special thank-you to the many people and teams that were willing to be interviewed and that invited me into their creative process. Your insights were invaluable, and your willingness to share them will enable so many others to serve as leaders of remarkable ideas.

Most important, I am grateful to my family—especially my wife, Erica; my parents, Nancy and Mark; my sisters, Gila and Julie; Susan Kaplan; and Alain, Ellen, and Remy Roizen—all of whom provided endless encouragement over the years as I labored through my own journey to make ideas happen. I also wish to thank my grandfather, Stanley Kaplan, a man who was also motivated to help people achieve their true potential, for the inspiration and important lessons his life provided.

Appendix 1:
Tips for Practicing the Action Method

Design for the Action Method

Regardless of what type of notebook or journal you use, you should consider designating certain spaces for actionable items and Backburner Items. These spaces should be kept separate from the space you use for general notes and sketching. Here is an example of how we practice the Action Method using the products we designed.

Online Utilities for the Action Method

The concept of the Action Method can be practiced using most online task management tools. There are many options for project management, but I encourage you to select one with an emphasis on action. Wunderlist is a common favorite for individuals, and Asana is used by many teams that work with a bias toward action. Keep experimenting and optimizing your system over time.

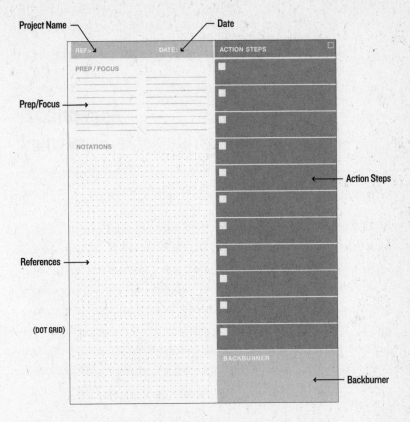

Project Name

Date

Prep/Focus

References

(DOT GRID)

Action Steps

Backburner

REF:

DATE:

ACTION STEPS

PREP / FOCUS

NOTATIONS

BACKBURNER

The Action Method design that the Behance team uses in meetings and brainstorms

More Resources on Action and Execution

Behance's annual 99U Conference and database of tips, interviews, and other resources are organized online and can be accessed at 99U.com. The 99U also functions as a community of like-minded creative people and teams with the desire to exchange best practices and boost productivity. You are welcome to participate.

Appendix 2:
The Purple Santa Experiment

AS AN EXPLORATION in rapid idea generation turned execution (and for the purpose of holiday cheer), the Behance team conducted a fun experiment in 2008. On one mid-December afternoon, the Behance team gathered around a table in our old start-up office to enjoy some lunch. Like at most lunches in the early days, we were brimming with ideas for what Behance might become and how organized the creative world should be (and what we could do to make it happen). And then our conversations would take drastic turns, to dream travel spots, childhood stories, and the occasional crazy idea that was tangential (at best) to our day jobs. One such idea was the concept of spreading holiday cheer. It was December 2008 and, amidst the looming recession, many of our friends across industries feared the worst. Layoffs were imminent.

Our meandering lunch discussion turned to the prospect of how to spread holiday happiness. And then the spark happened. "What if Santa made a surprise visit to a string of agencies and creative work spaces around New York City?"

One Santa became three purple Santas with long purple beards, large red bags full of candy, lottery scratch tickets, and little notes inspiring holiday cheer. It was just one of those crazy fledgling ideas that was unlikely to ever see the light of day. But for some reason, it started to gain traction, and some granularity emerged over the course of the conversation. There was the proposed policy about anonymity (we wouldn't tell people we were doing it; our strategy for dealing with security guards); we would explain that we were sent to deliver Christmas cheer to someone we knew in each agency; and we agreed to keep the budget minimal. The idea was getting some legs.

After forty minutes, we realized that the time set aside for lunch had long passed. People started to gather their crumbs and take the last sip before returning to ongoing projects and the daily tasks. The idea had nearly slipped away in a matter of minutes. And then, right before we all broke in our own directions, one team member said, "Hey, I know where we can get really cheap Santa outfits with white beards that could easily be died purple." Alas, a proposed Action Step!

Rather than create a project plan and really put our minds to-gether around the project—something that we just didn't have the time to do—the team decided to simply act on the idea without much thought. Rather than plan, we decided to rapidly propose, assign, and take a series of actions to see if this fledgling idea could actually hap-pen without any formal process. Of course, the risk for the idea was low. The cost of three unused Santa costumes and excess office candy was one we were willing to incur. But there was also a desire to test ourselves, not to mention the fact that the prospect of spreading holiday cheer was fun and rewarding in itself.

And so, in a quick series of actions taken, PurpleSanta.com was purchased and developed in twenty minutes, the costumes were pur-chased, the beards were dyed, and the team was ready one afternoon for Operation Purple Santa. The actual Purple Santas—who shall remain anonymous—visited seven different companies. There were Twitter and Facebook messages about the strange Purple Santas running through offices. Others began broadcasting a call out into the ether, pleading for the Purple Santas to visit their office as well.

In this experiment, a random idea thrived only through a willingness to act quickly and *without* conviction. This fond memory serves to illustrate the mechanics of quick action and how, without it, fledgling ideas are far less likely to ever happen.

Appendix 3:
Overview of the Behance Network

THE BEHANCE NETWORK is a free platform for the world's leading creative professionals. Behance.net is used mostly by professionals in the visual creative industries—including designers, photographers, illustrators, and all kinds of other artists—as a powerful tool to showcase their world broadly, solicit feedback, and build a professional network. Millions of people visit the Behance Network and its affiliated sites every month to explore, find, and hire top creative talent.

Our team developed the Behance Network as a means of fostering accountability, career development, and knowledge exchange in the creative professional community. It is designed to help organize the creative world's work. The Network's utilities, design, and extensive partnerships empower creative professionals to lead their own careers. The Network has also become one of the best recruiting spots for companies to search for and hire top talent.

You are welcome to visit the Behance Network at behance.net—whether for inspiration, to find and hire top talent, or with the intention to showcase your own creative work.

Index

About the Author

SCOTT BELSKY BELIEVES that the greatest breakthroughs across all industries are a result of creative people and teams that are especially productive. As such, Scott has committed his professional life to helping organize creative people, teams, and networks.

Scott is the founder and CEO of Behance, a company that develops products and services to organize the creative world. He also leads "The 99%," Behance's think tank and annual conference that conducts and showcases research on organization and execution in the creative world.

Behance's first product, the Behance Network, has become the leading online platform for creative professionals. The Network collectively receives millions of visitors every month and has become one of the most efficient platforms for creative professionals to broadcast their work to top agencies, fans, peers, and recruiters.

In 2008, Behance launched the Action Method, a revolutionary "action management" system that has replaced traditional project management practices throughout the creative professional world and beyond. Behance also developed the Action Method product line—a series of organizational products that are sold around the world.

Scott has traveled the globe meeting with hundreds of creative professionals and teams, always asking the question, "How do you make ideas happen?" He has consulted for leading media companies, helped institute work flow changes at top advertising agencies, and regularly speaks at major conferences in the creative industries. He has also shared Behance's research in segments on ABC News and MSNBC, and is a regular contributor on American Express's Open Forum.

Prior to founding Behance, Scott helped grow the Pine Street Leadership Development Initiative at the Goldman Sachs Group, Inc. He was especially focused on organizational improvement and strengthening relationships with key clients.

Scott also hopes to increase "productive creativity" in the not-for-profit world through his involvement on various boards, including Cornell University's Entrepreneurship Program and Reboot.

Scott's education is in design, environmental economics, and business. He attended Cornell University as an undergraduate and received his MBA from Harvard Business School.

Scott lives and works in New York City.

CONNECT WITH SCOTT:
www.scottbelsky.com
twitter.com/scottbelsky